LOVE & VERMIN

ALSO BY WILL McPHAIL

IN: A GRAPHIC NOVEL

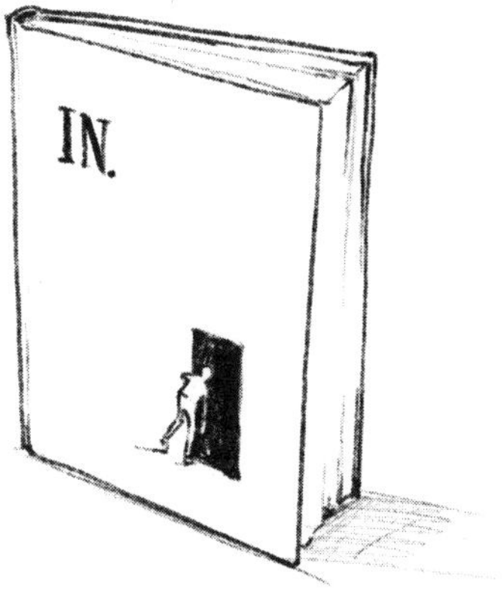
IN.

LOVE & VERMIN

A Collection of Cartoons
by *The New Yorker's*

WILL McPHAIL

MARINER BOOKS

New York Boston

HARPERCOLLINS BOOKS MAY BE PURCHASED FOR EDUCATIONAL, BUSINESS, OR SALES PROMOTIONAL USE. FOR INFORMATION, PLEASE EMAIL THE SPECIAL MARKETS DEPARTMENT AT SPSALES@HARPERCOLLINS.COM.

FIRST EDITION

DESIGNED BY CHLOE FOSTER

LIBRARY OF CONGRESS CONTROL NUMBER: 2022942323

ISBN 978-0-358-34622-7

22 23 24 25 26 LSC 10 9 8 7 6 5 4 3 2 1

CALVIN

Isn't it strange that evolution would give us a sense of humor?

When you think about it, it's weird that we have a physiological response to absurdity. We _laugh_ at nonsense. We _like_ it. We think it's funny.

Don't you think it's odd that we _appreciate_ absurdity? Why would we develop that way? How does it benefit us?

HOBBES

I suppose if we couldn't laugh at things that don't make sense, we couldn't react to a lot of life.

CALVIN

I can't tell if that's funny or really scary.

— BILL WATTERSON

CONTENTS

LOVE & VERMIN

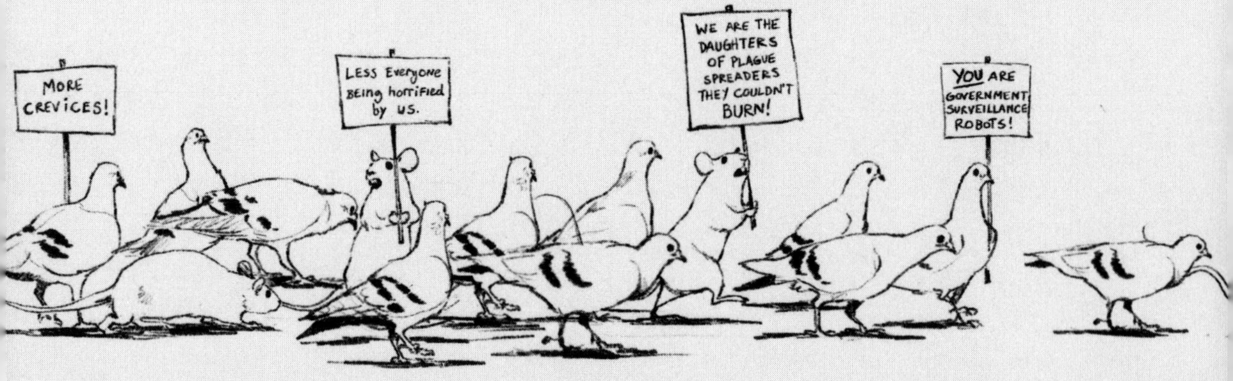

MORE CREVICES!
LESS Everyone Being horrified by us.
WE ARE THE DAUGHTERS OF PLAGUE SPREADERS THEY COULDN'T BURN!
YOU ARE GOVERNMENT SURVEILLANCE ROBOTS!

1

MY BRAVE LITTLE OPINIONS

I'LL OFTEN USE CARTOONS AS A WAY TO WORK OUT MY VIEWS ON THE WORLD. GENERALLY, I'M AN IDIOT WHO NEEDS TO HAVE OPINIONS DICTATED TO HIM BY SMARTER PEOPLE ON TWITTER. BUT IF I CAN GET THE TANGLED THREADS OF A SOCIAL OR POLITICAL ISSUE STRAIGHT ON PAPER, THEN I CAN GET THEM STRAIGHT IN MY HEAD. IN A STRANGE WAY, WORKING OUT HOW TO JOKE ABOUT SOMETHING FORCES YOU TO DECIDE WHICH SIDE YOU'RE ON.

A FUNNY SIDE EFFECT OF DOING THESE KINDS OF CARTOONS IS THAT SOME PEOPLE SEE ONE OF THEM AND ASSUME THAT I'M ALWAYS MAKING A POLITICAL POINT. I CAN'T DRAW AN AVOCADO NOW WITHOUT A BUNCH OF PEOPLE FIGHTING IN THE COMMENTS ABOUT WHETHER THE AVOCADO REPRESENTS REPRODUCTIVE RIGHTS OR SCOTTISH INDEPENDENCE.

BOOO!

SORRY, WE CAN'T
OPEN JARS.

"I SAID, 'I WONDER WHAT IT MEANS,'
NOT 'TELL ME WHAT IT MEANS.'"

"LISTEN TO ME. GENDER IS A CONSTRUCT,
SOCIETY IS A CONSTRUCT, MONEY IS A CONSTRUCT.
BUT BEDTIME IS VERY, VERY REAL."

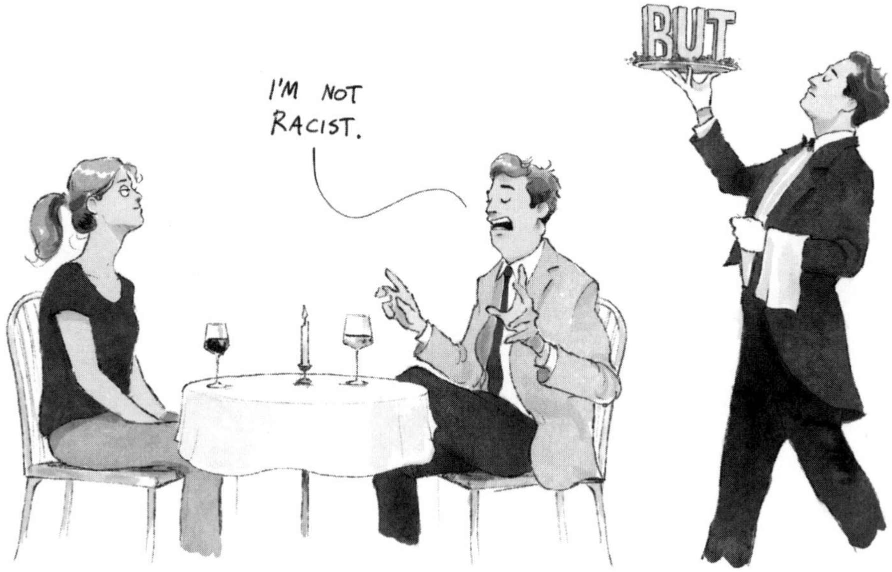
I'M NOT RACIST.
BUT

"DESCRIBE WHAT YOU CAN BRING TO THIS COMPANY."

"THESE SMUG PILOTS HAVE LOST TOUCH WITH
REGULAR PASSENGERS LIKE US.
WHO THINKS I SHOULD FLY THE PLANE?"

"YOUR RÉSUMÉ MENTIONS A PENIS. TELL US ABOUT THAT."

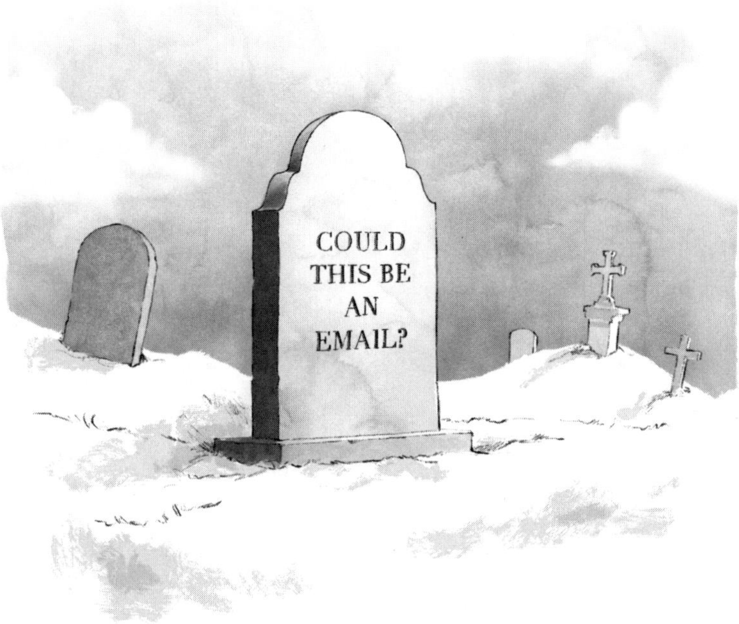
COULD
THIS BE
AN
EMAIL?

"COULD YOU NOT DO THAT? KEEPING BABIES ALIVE
IN PUBLIC MAKES ME UNCOMFORTABLE."

"IF YOU KEEP PLAYING WITH THOSE DOLLS, YOU'LL GROW UP
NOTHING LIKE ME. IS THAT WHAT YOU WANT?"

"I SWEAR IF ONE MORE OF MY HEROES LETS ME DOWN,
I'M GONNA REALIZE THAT THEY'RE ALL MEN."

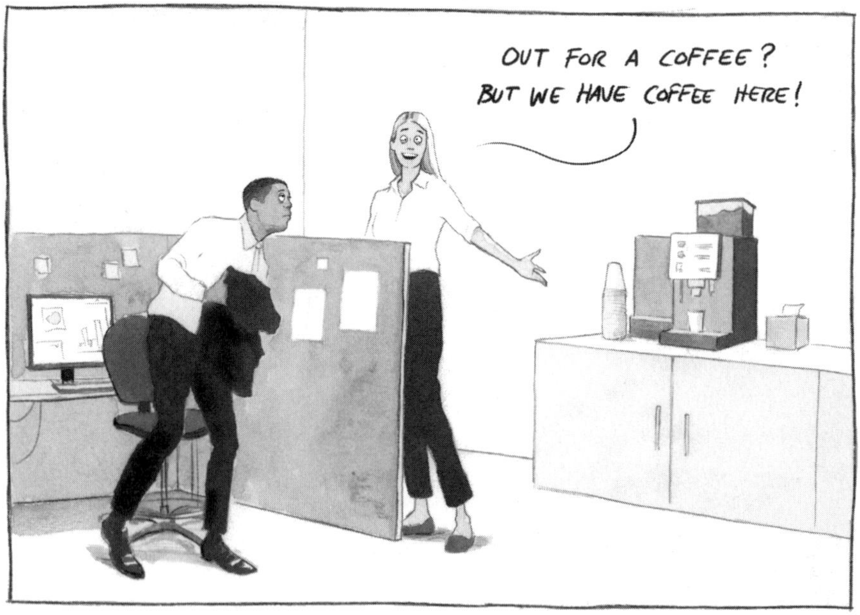
OUT FOR A COFFEE? BUT WE HAVE COFFEE HERE!

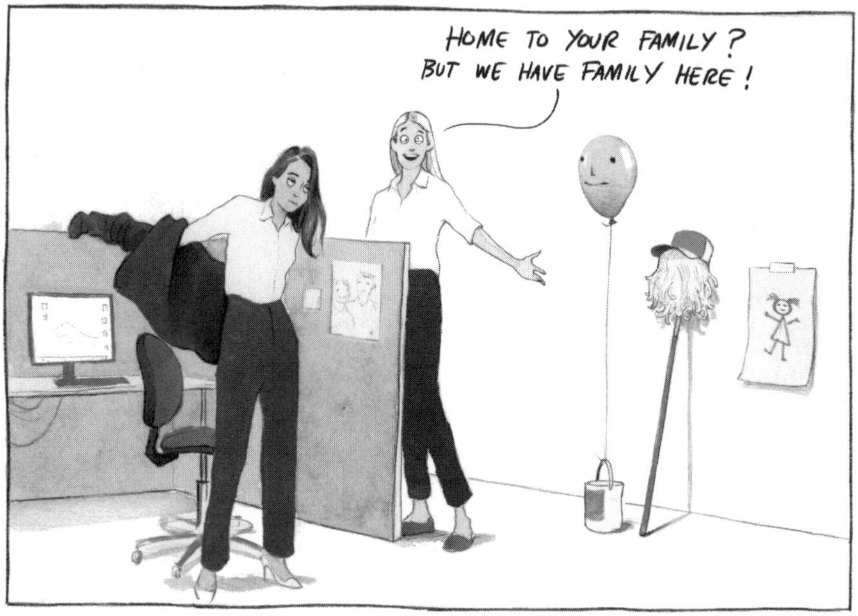
HOME TO YOUR FAMILY? BUT WE HAVE FAMILY HERE!

Panning For Sense

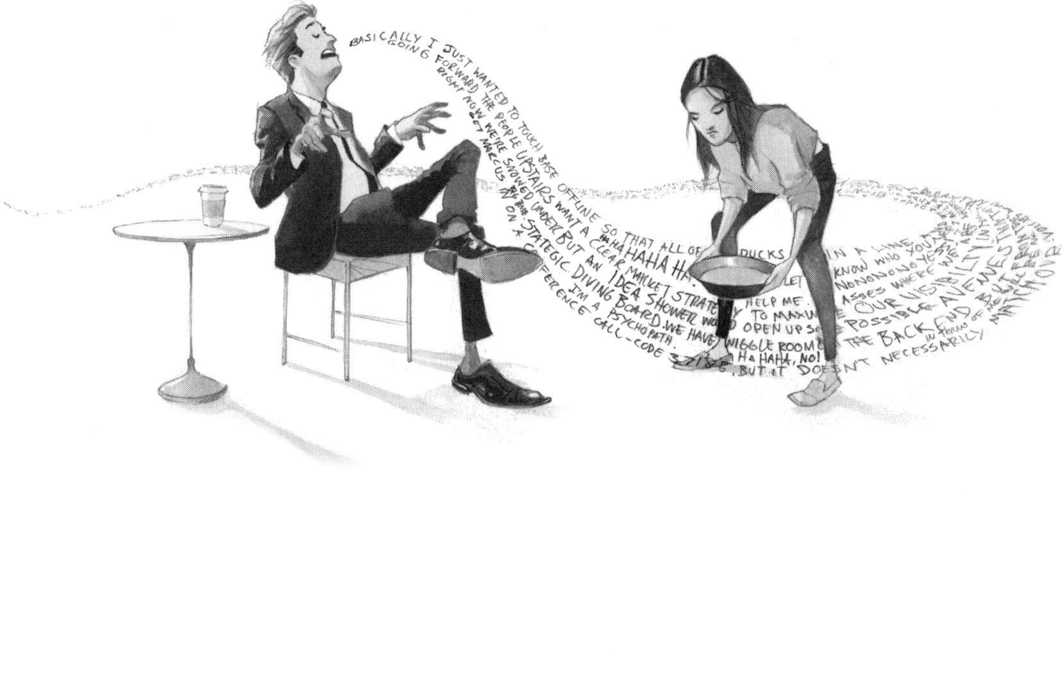

BASICALLY I JUST WANTED TO TOUCH BASE OFFLINE SO THAT ALL OF
DUCKS
IN A LINE
GOING FORWARD THE PEOPLE UPSTAIRS WANT A CLEAR MARKET STRATE
HELP ME.
TO MAXIM
RIGHT NOW WE'RE SNOWED UNDER BUT AN IDEA SHOWER WO
OPEN UP SO
GET MARCUS ON A STRATEGIC DIVING BOARD. WE HAVE
WIGGLE ROOM
HAHAHA HA
LET
KNOW WHO YOU
NONONONO YES
ASSES WHERE WE
OUR VISIBILITY
POSSIBLE AVENUES
THE BACK END
IN TERMS OF
NECESSARILY
I'M A PSYCHOPATH.
HA HAHA, NO!
CONFERENCE CALL-CODE
BUT IT DOESN'T

"HEY, GOD? CAN WE MAKE EVE NOW?"

NO IS AN ANSWER

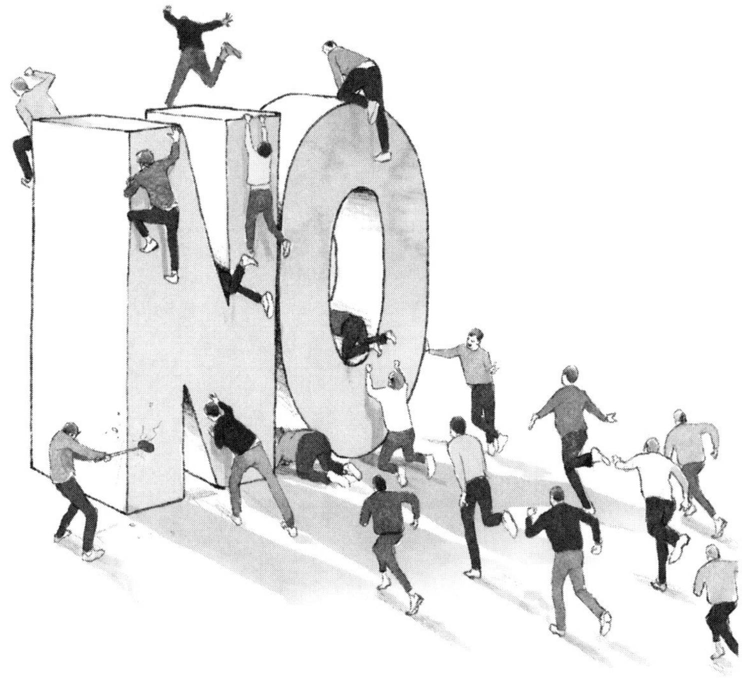
NO

NOT AN OBSTACLE.

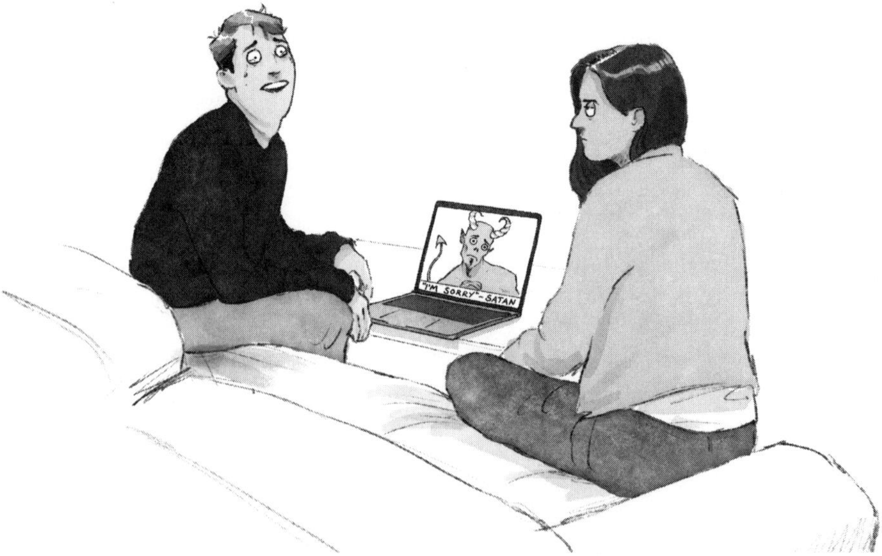
"I'M SORRY"-SATAN

"BUT HIS APOLOGY VIDEO IS SO GENUINE!"

"HEY, DUDE, THE FIFTIES CALLED: THEY WANT THEIR SHIRT BACK.
THEY ALSO SAID THAT THINGS ARE PRETTY TOUGH THERE.
KIND OF A SAD CALL, ACTUALLY."

"RIGHT, BUT IF YOU THINK ABOUT <u>ANYTHING</u> FOR
LONG ENOUGH, THEN I'M WRONG."

"BEHOLD, AS I TRANSFORM THIS NORMAL WOMAN
INTO A SEXUALIZED PROP."

EVOLUTION OF MAN

"OK, ABIRDTOOKMYSON.COM IS TAKEN.
I'LL TRY .BIZ."

"WHEN I GET A BRAIN, I'M GONNA FIGURE OUT IF IT'S COOL FOR THREE DUDES TO FOLLOW A LITTLE GIRL THROUGH THE WOODS."

"WHY WOULD YOU MAKE BELIEVE THEY'RE BEHIND ON MORTGAGE PAYMENTS?"

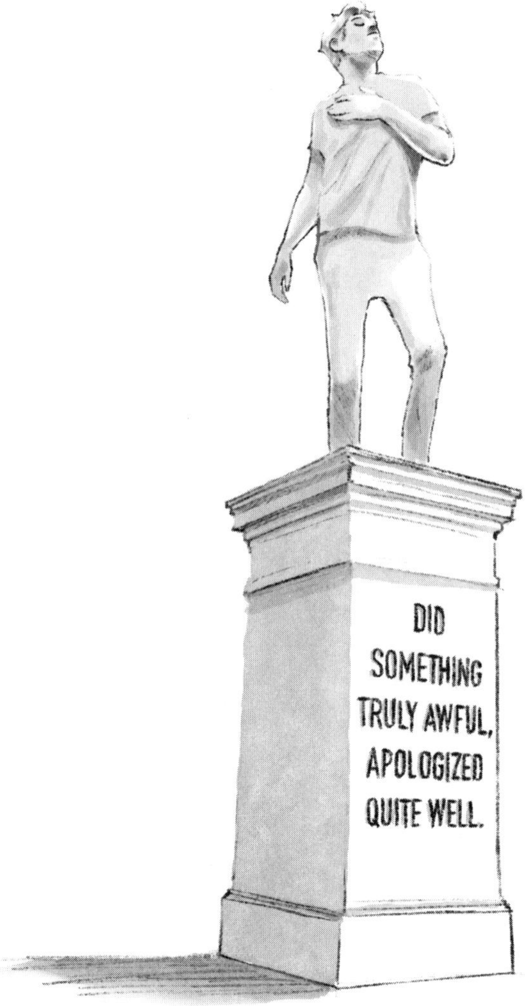
DID
SOMETHING
TRULY AWFUL,
APOLOGIZED
QUITE WELL.

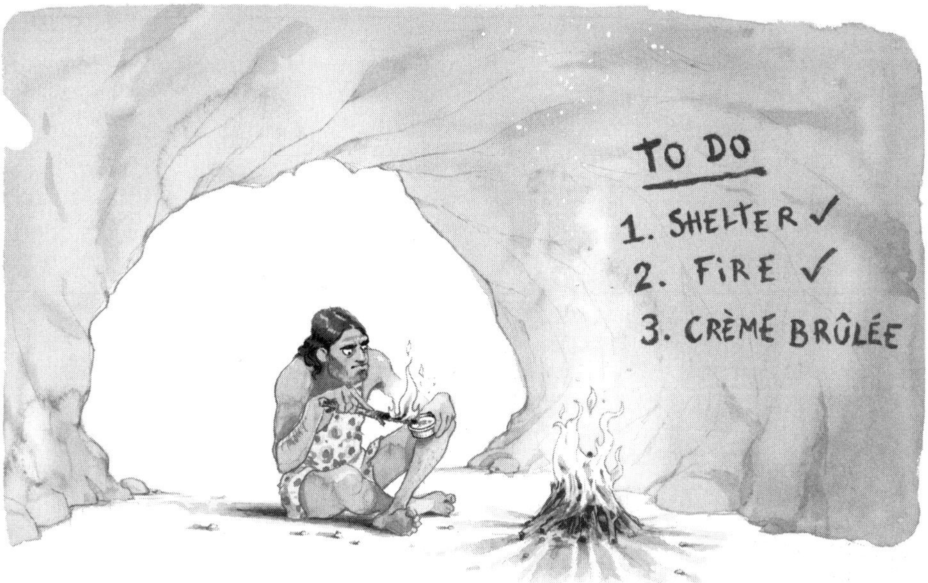
TO DO
1. SHELTER ✓
2. FIRE ✓
3. CRÈME BRÛLÉE

A FOOLPROOF GUIDE TO ACHIEVING LITERARY SUCCESS

I SEE YOU PURCHASED A NOTEPAD! HERE, HAVE A BOOK DEAL.
EXCELLENT. I DESERVE THIS.
Book Deal
YOU DO.
AND YOU DON'T NEED TO SEE ANY ACTUAL WORK BECAUSE...
BECAUSE IT'S CLEAR FROM YOUR DEDICATION TO STATIONERY THAT YOU ARE A SERIOUS ARTIST WHOSE WORK TRANSCENDS TIME, GENDER, AND RACE.
OF COURSE.
OF COURSE.
YOU KNOW I ALMOST DID SOME WORK BEFORE YOU CAME.
YOU BOUGHT THE NOTEPAD! THAT'S ALL THE WORK YOU NEED TO DO RIGHT NOW.

OR EVER?
OR EVER!
HA HA HA HA HA
COME TO THE MOUNTAINS.

YOUR EX IS JEALOUS OF YOU.

2

VERMIN

WHY AM I SO OBSESSED WITH RATS AND PIGEONS? SCIENTISTS ARE BAFFLED BY ME. I THINK IT'S BECAUSE THEY'RE CREEPY AND THEY'RE DESPERATE AND THEY'RE BAD TO LOOK AT, WHICH IS A BRAVE CHOICE IN THIS IMAGE-OBSESSED WORLD. THEY WARM MY HEART AND TURN MY STOMACH ALL AT ONCE, AND I'VE ALWAYS FOUND THAT TO BE A VERY FUNNY COMBO. MOST OF ALL, I JUST DON'T KNOW WHY THEY WANT TO BE HERE! I LIVE IN THE SQUALOR OF A CITY BECAUSE IT MEANS I CAN GO ON HOT DATES AND SIT IN COOL COFFEE SHOPS, BUT WHAT ARE PIGEONS DOING HERE THAT THEY COULDN'T DO FAR AWAY IN THE BEAUTIFUL COUNTRYSIDE? EITHER WAY, I FEEL AN OBLIGATION TO BE KIND TO THEM NOW BECAUSE I'VE ESSENTIALLY BUILT A CAREER OFF DRAWING THEM.

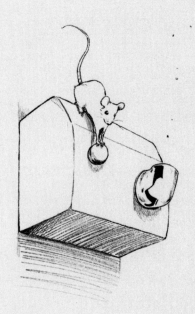

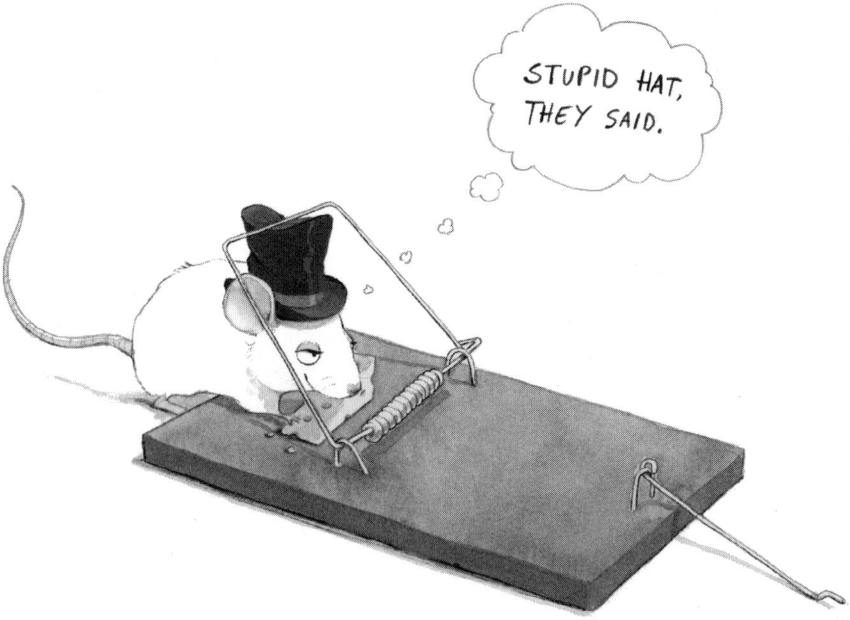
STUPID HAT,
THEY SAID.

THEY LOVE ME.

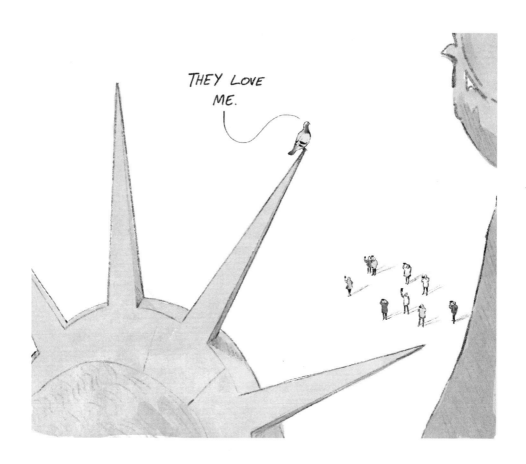

"SHOWTIME."

"IT KEEPS THE GUYS AWAY."

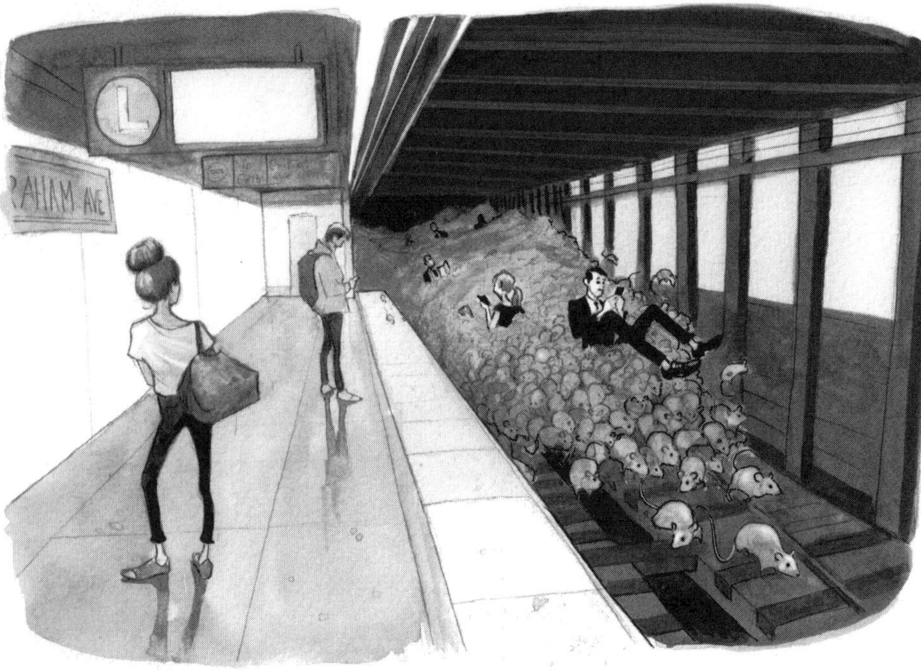
L
RAHAM AVE

"DUE TO A POWER LOSS, THIS TRAIN WILL BE REPLACED BY A WAVE OF RATS."

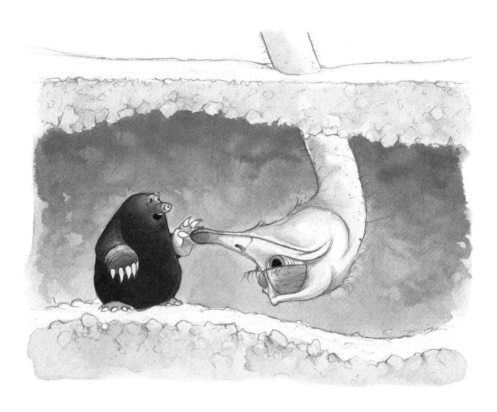

"YOU CAN'T HIDE OUR RELATIONSHIP FOREVER."

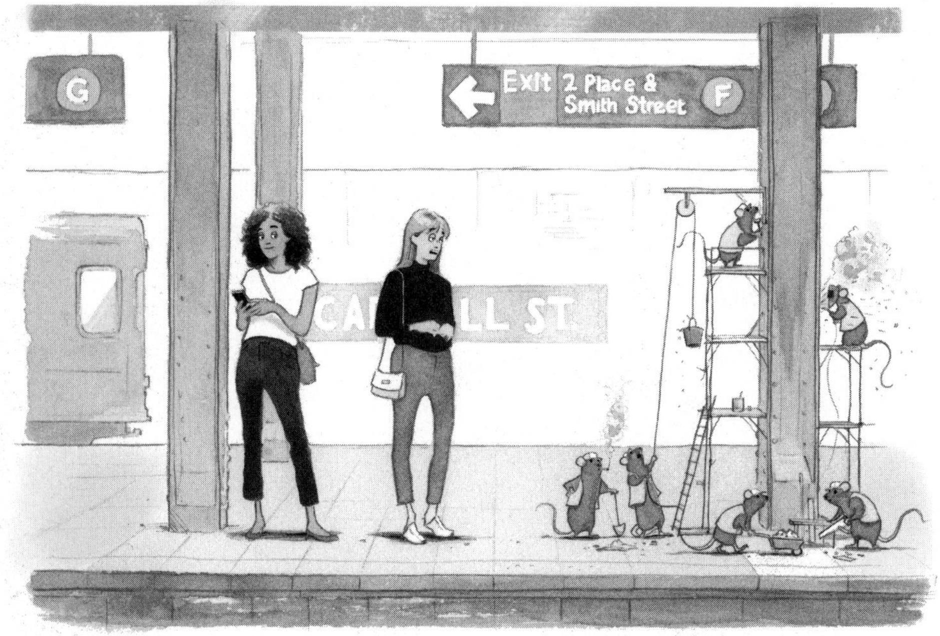
G
Exit
2 Place &
Smith Street
F

"AT LEAST SOMEONE CARES ABOUT THIS PLACE."

"DO YOU EVER WISH THAT A DIFFERENT PLACE FELT LIKE HOME?"

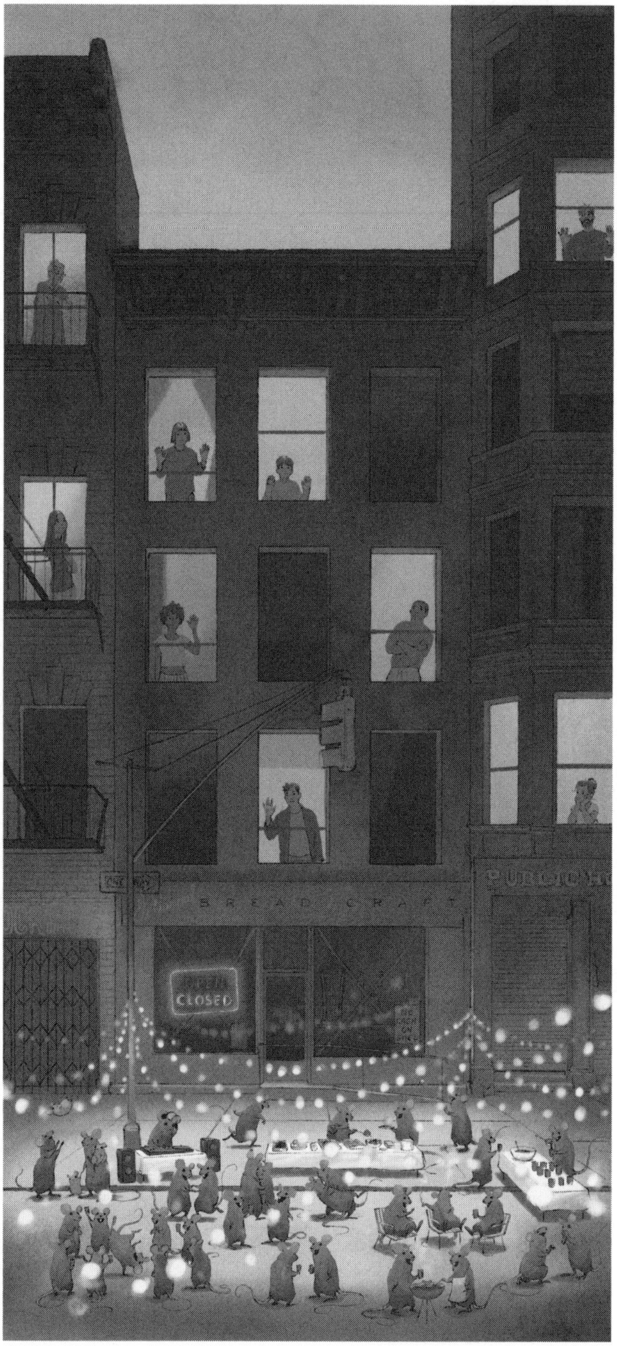
BREAD CRAFT
CLOSED

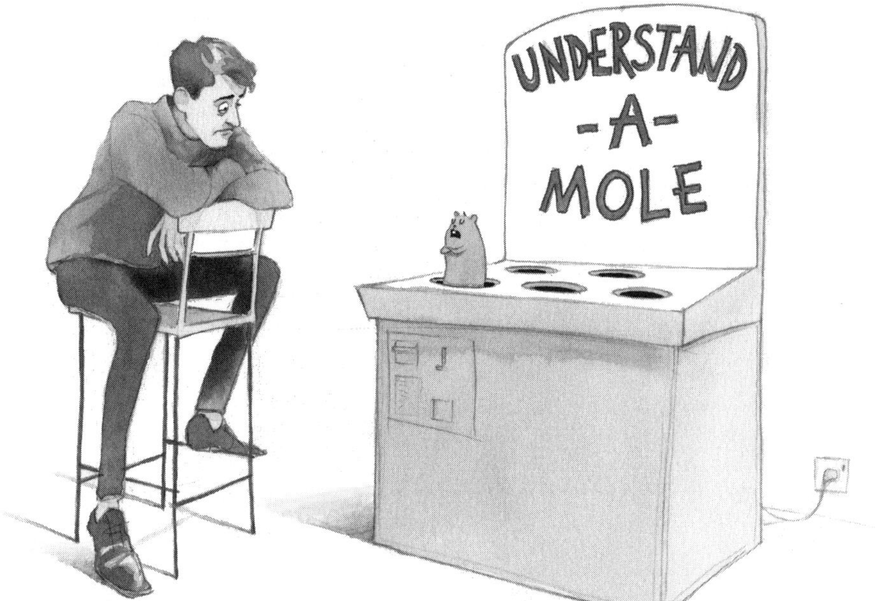
UNDERSTAND
-A-
MOLE

NICE JACKET.
THANK YOU.
BE A SHAME IF SOMETHING WERE TO HAPPEN TO IT.
LEAVE THE CHIPS.

"THE PIGEON KING GROWS TIRED OF YOUR
CAREER ADVICE, MOTHER."

"NOW _THIS_ IS HUMANE."

"BAD NEWS—THE RATS ARE SUBLETTING TO COCKROACHES."

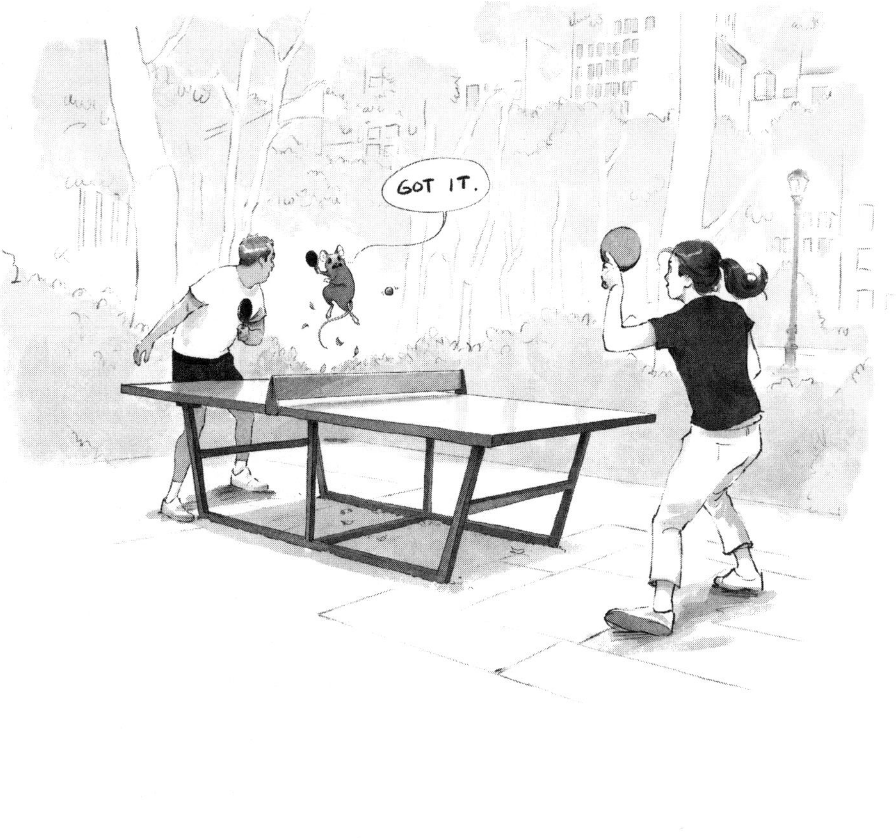
GOT IT.

"IF I GIVE YOU THE JOB, WILL YOU TELL ME
HOW YOU KEEP GETTING IN HERE?"

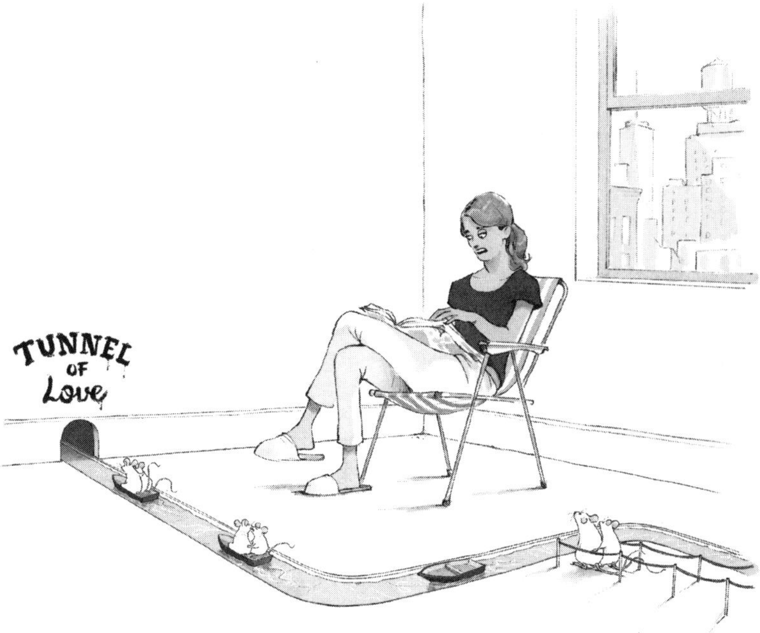
TUNNEL OF Love

"TEN DOLLARS."

NYC'S MOST ELIGIBLE PIGEONS

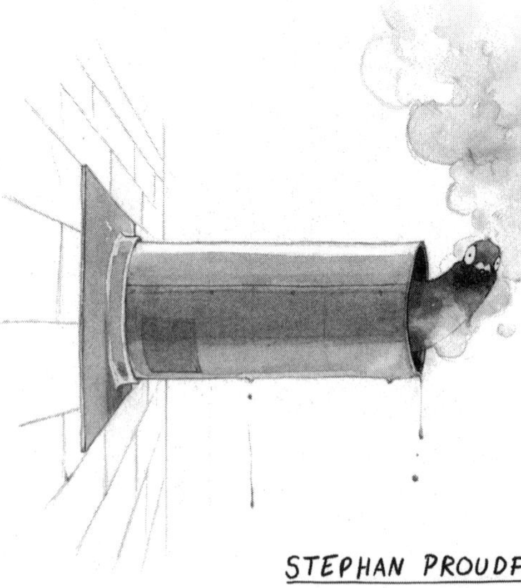

FRANCIS FAIRFEATHER

THIS REAL-ESTATE MOGUL HAS PROPERTY IN THE DELI PIPE THAT BLASTS OUT MEAT WIND, THE GAP IN THE TRAIN PLATFORM—BASICALLY, WHEREVER PEOPLE DIDN'T CARE ENOUGH TO PUT SPIKES.

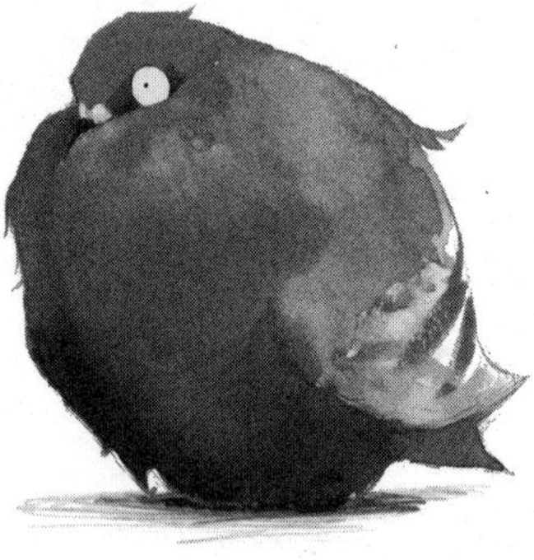

STEPHAN PROUDFOOT

BIRD-ABOUT-TOWN STEPHAN IS ONE OF THOSE NOT-QUITE-AS-HIDEOUS BROWN ONES.

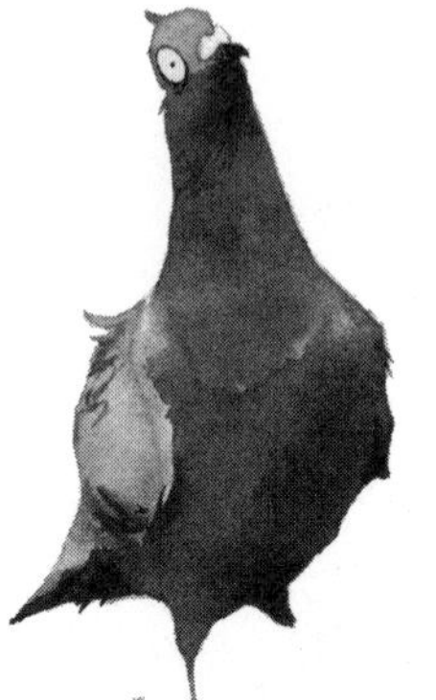

DAVID HORNBY-WENNING

LIKE ACCENTS? DAVID GREW UP ON THE LEAFY STREETS OF LONDON AND IS HEIR TO A VAST BISCUIT FORTUNE (ONE BISCUIT).
DON'T LIKE ACCENTS? COOL, HE CAN'T TALK.

CLARKE ST. BRANCH

CLARKE'S LIST OF CELEBRITY
ROMANCES INCLUDES THE PIGEON
THAT RACHEL TRAPPED IN A POT
ON <u>FRIENDS</u> AND THE EAGLE
THAT SCARED TRUMP.

CLAUDIO WHEATLEAF

ENTREPRENEUR CLAUDIO CROWDFUNDED A
PILE OF SEEDS AT THE TENDER AGE OF
FEATHERLESS AND BLIND. LOCK UP YOUR
DAUGHTERS, BECAUSE THIS LOTHARIO
MATES FOR LIFE (AROUND SIX YEARS).

BENEDICT ELDERBERRY

HELD A HIGH-LEVEL POSITION ON WALL STREET
UNTIL SOMEONE SHOOED HIM AWAY. NOW BENEDICT
SPENDS MOST OF HIS TIME IN THE GLORIOUS
UPSTATE COUNTRYSIDE, BECAUSE WHY DOESN'T EVERY
PIGEON DO THAT? THEY CAN JUST DO THAT.

3

LESSER ANIMALS

I STUDIED ZOOLOGY AT UNIVERSITY, BECAUSE WHEN YOU ASK A SEVENTEEN-YEAR-OLD CHILD WHAT THE ADULT VERSION OF HIMSELF WILL WANT TO DO UNTIL HE'S BECOME THE DEAD VERSION OF HIMSELF, HE ALWAYS MAKES A PERFECT DECISION. I'M FASCINATED BY ANIMALS, BUT I WAS NEVER REALLY INVESTED ACADEMICALLY, SO DURING LECTURES I WOULD FILL MY NOTES WITH INSANE DOODLES INSTEAD OF WHATEVER MY LECTURER WAS TALKING ABOUT—BARNACLES, USUALLY. BARNACLES WERE A HUGE PART OF MY LIFE FOR AN UNEXPECTED AMOUNT OF TIME.

PEOPLE TELL ME THAT THE THIRTY THOUSAND GREAT BRITISH POUNDS I SPENT ON THE COURSE WEREN'T COMPLETELY WASTED, BECAUSE NOW I DRAW A LOT OF ANIMALS IN MY CARTOONS, BUT I'M NOT SURE. HONESTLY, I THINK I MIGHT BE DRAWING THEM ONLY TO RETROACTIVELY MAKE MY DEGREE SEEM MORE WORTHWHILE. LIKE IF I DRAW A PICTURE OF A SLUG THIS AFTERNOON, THEN SOMEHOW THAT WILL MAKE THOSE FOUR YEARS OF AWKWARD SEX AND MOLDY SHOWER CURTAINS ALL WORTH IT.

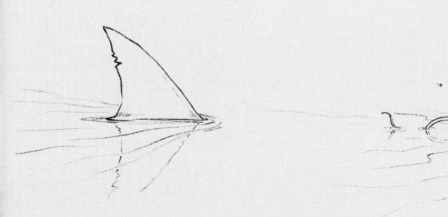

"YOU KNOW WHAT DOESN'T GROW BACK, SUSAN? TRUST."

"OOH, NICE SERVE, MEGAN! HEY, CAN SOMEONE TELL
MEGAN TO COOL IT ON THE SERVE? HA HA,
JUST KIDDING, MEGAN. GREAT SERVE."

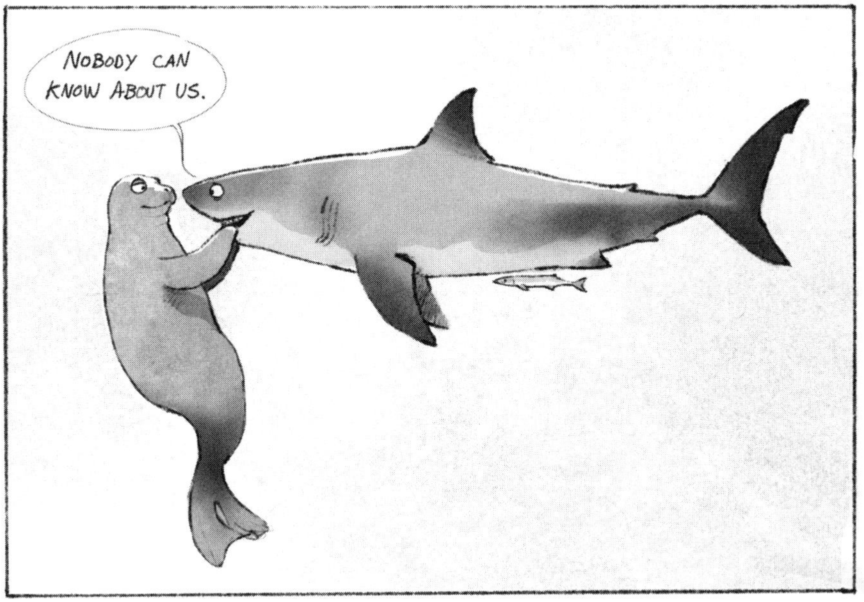
NOBODY CAN KNOW ABOUT US.

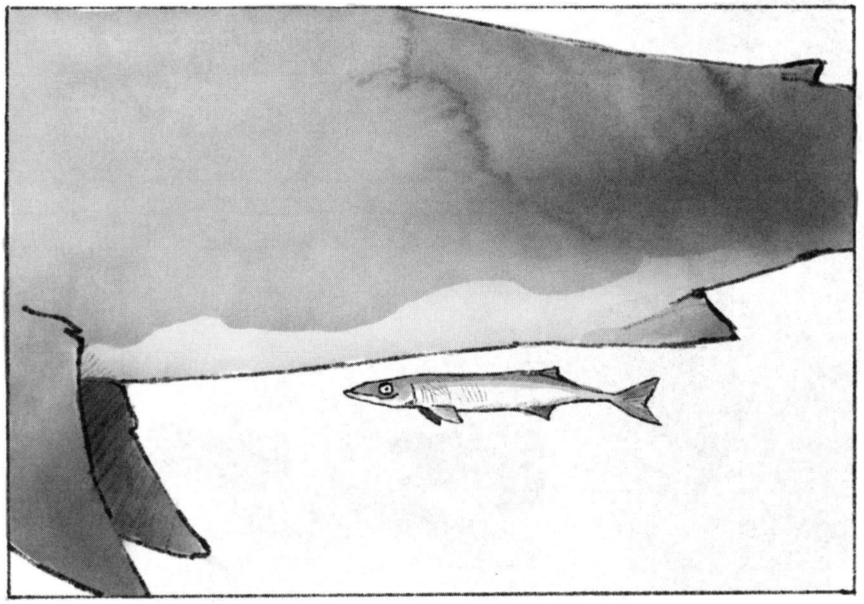

LATE BIRD HATES WORMS ANYWAY

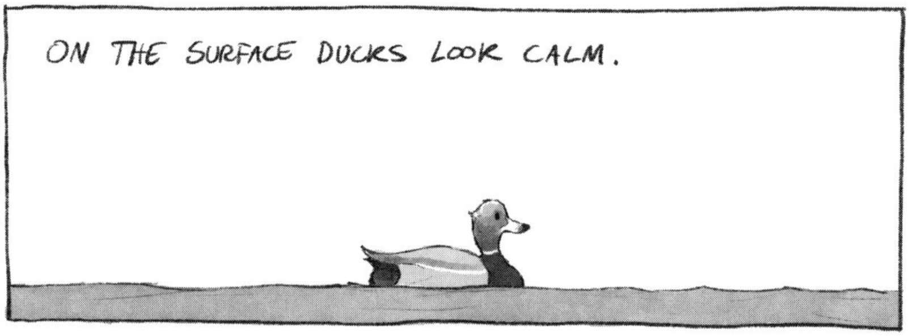
ON THE SURFACE DUCKS LOOK CALM.

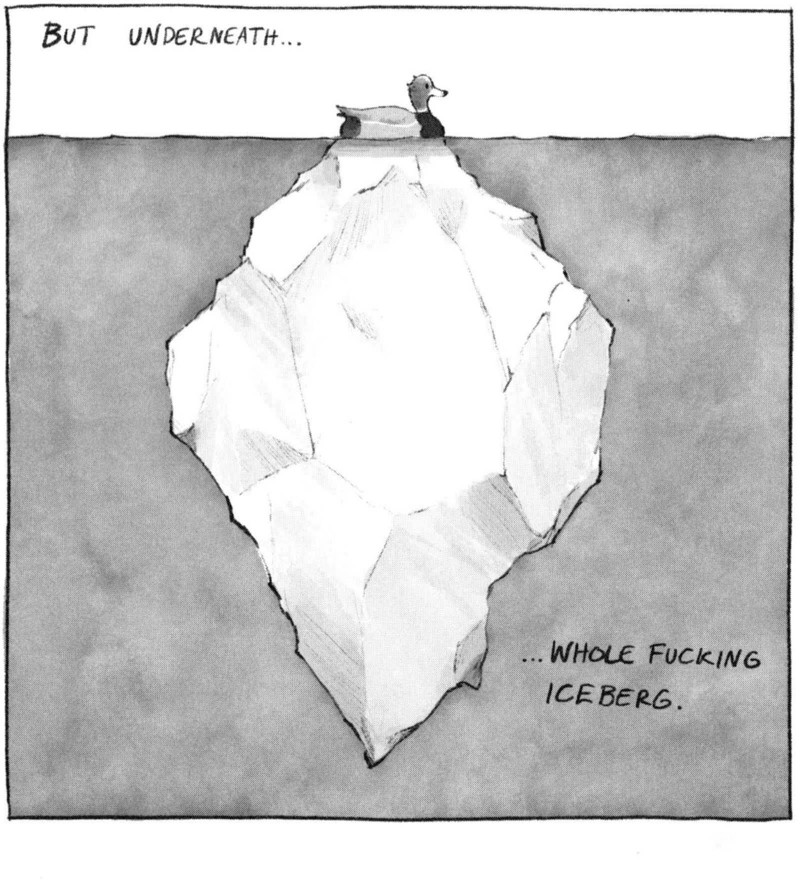
BUT UNDERNEATH...
...WHOLE FUCKING ICEBERG.

"I MEAN, IS THIS EVEN OUR STORY TO TELL?"

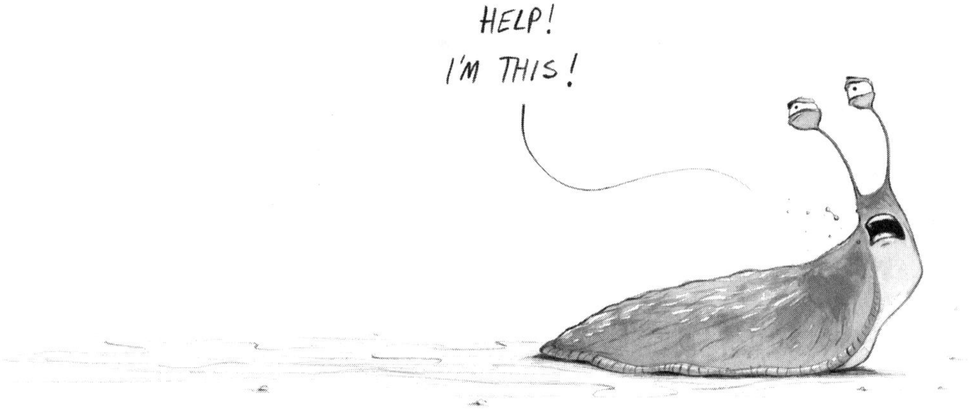
HELP!
I'M THIS!

"GUYS, THIS ISN'T WHAT I THOUGHT SWIMMING
WITH DOLPHINS WOULD BE LIKE."

"IS THIS TAKEN?"

"WHOA—I DIDN'T KNOW I COULD DO BEARS!"

"HEY, CAN YOU CLEAR MY SCHEDULE?"

My dearest Martha,

The rumors are true. I have
been eaten by an embarrassingly
small whale.

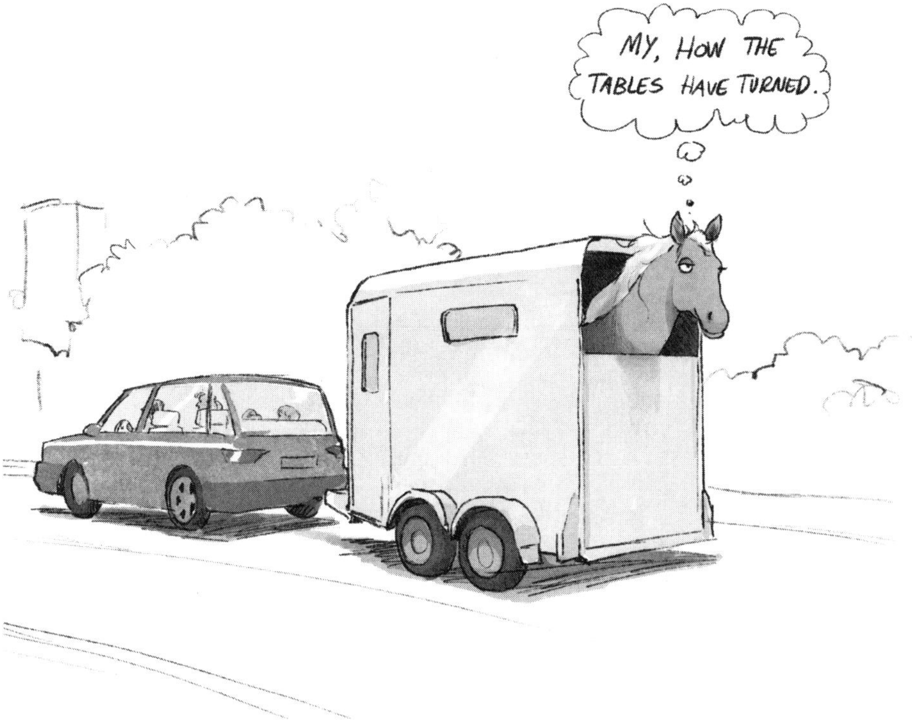
MY, HOW THE TABLES HAVE TURNED.

"THESE WHALE SOUNDS AREN'T CALMING ME DOWN AT ALL."

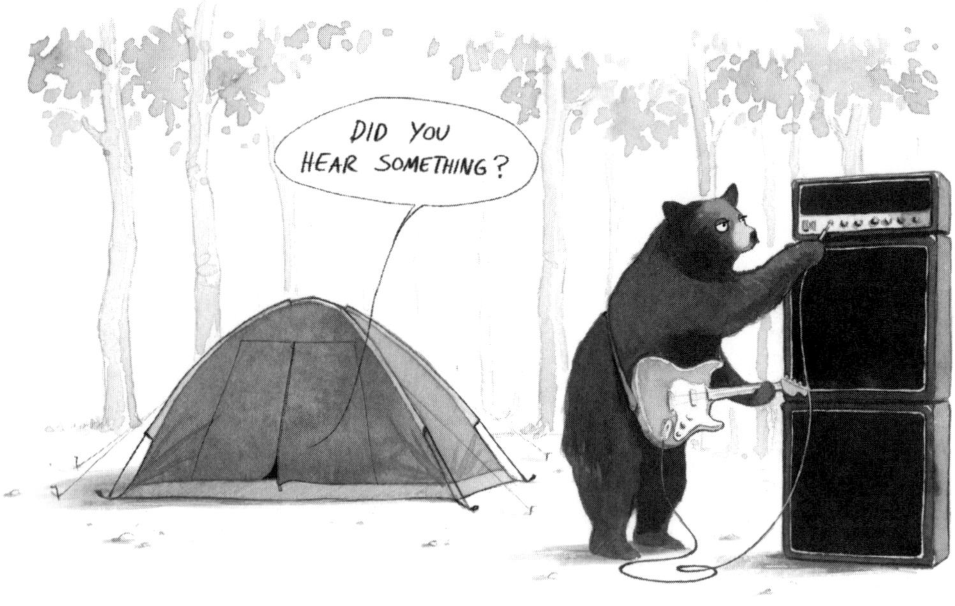
DID YOU HEAR SOMETHING?

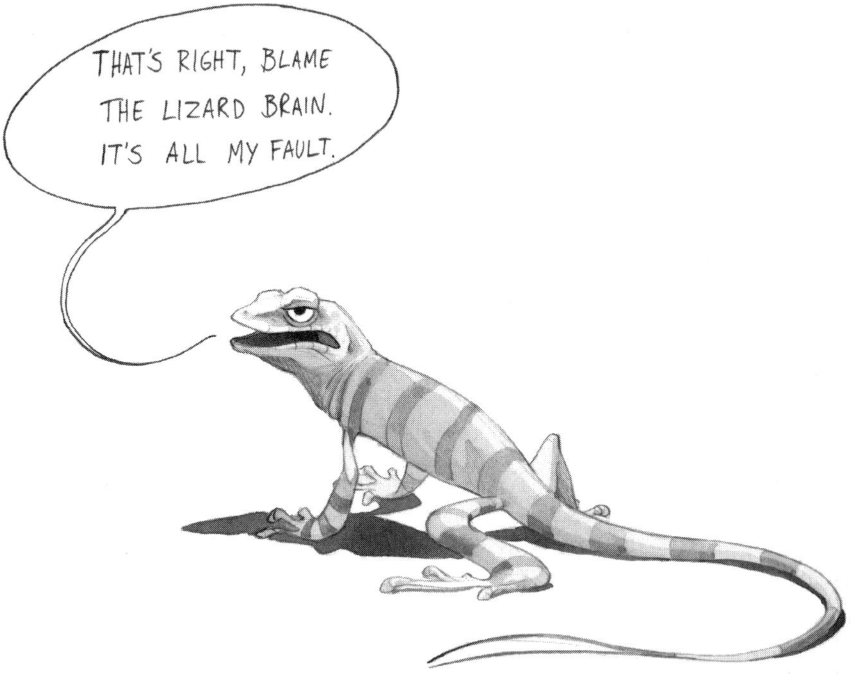
THAT'S RIGHT, BLAME THE LIZARD BRAIN. IT'S ALL MY FAULT.

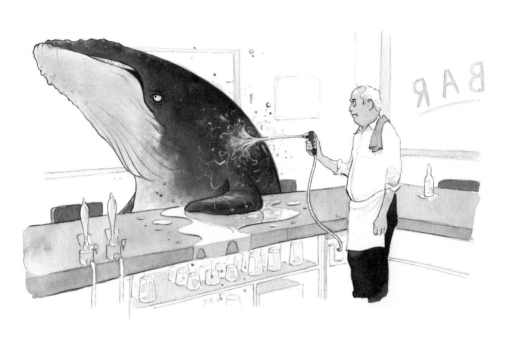

"I'LL TELL YOU WHEN I'VE HAD ENOUGH!"

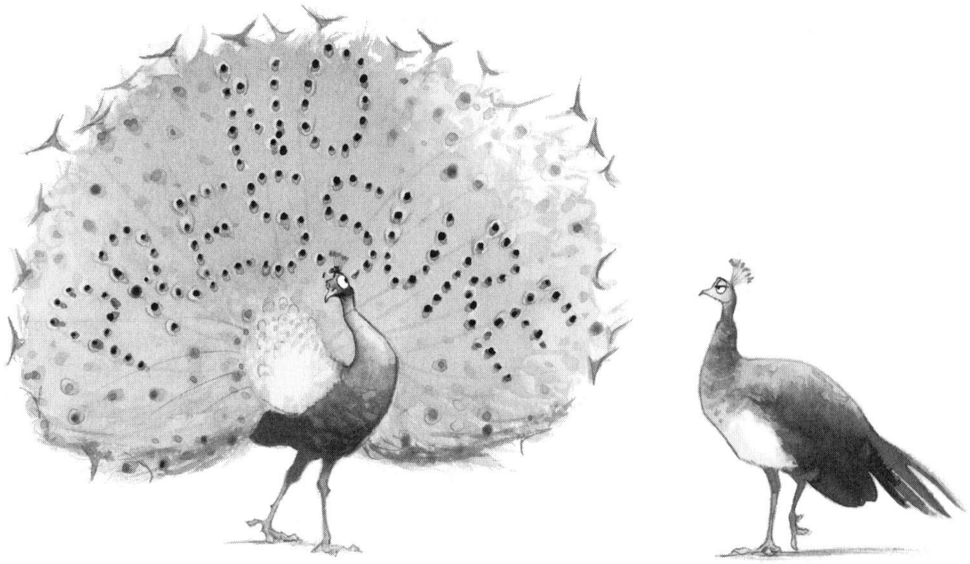
NO

"ALL RIGHT, WHAT DO YOU REALLY THINK OF IAN?"

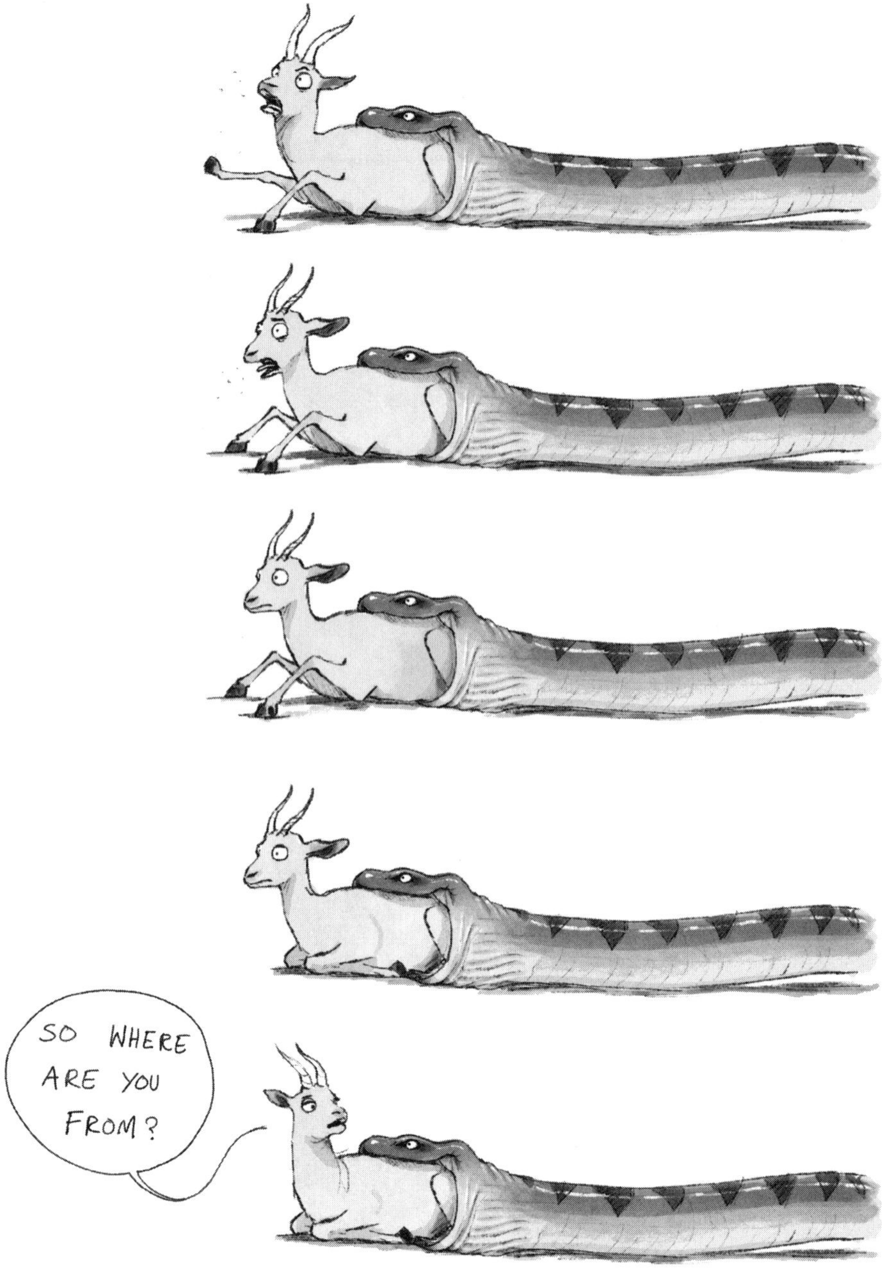
SO WHERE ARE YOU FROM?

"I THINK SOMEONE SPIT IN MY DRINK."

EVERYTHING IS GOING TO BE ALL RIGHT.
I DIDN'T SAY THAT.

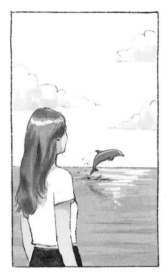

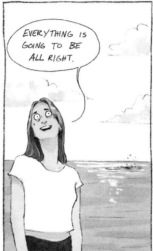

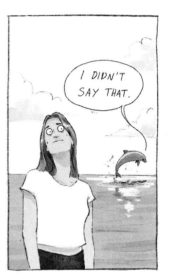

"YEAH, I'M GONNA HAVE TO CALL YOU BACK, DOCTOR."

"AND <u>THIS</u> FEATHER SHOWS THAT I WON'T INTERRUPT
YOU WHEN YOU'RE TALKING!"

4

NONSENSE

MY ABSOLUTE FAVORITE CARTOONS ARE THE ONES THAT MAKE ME LAUGH FOR A REASON I DON'T UNDERSTAND. THAT'S THE GOOD STUFF. AND WHEN YOU'VE ESSENTIALLY BUILT A LIFE AROUND GETTING REJECTED BY THE NEW YORKER'S EDITORS EVERY WEEK, THE CARTOONS THAT GENUINELY MAKE YOU LAUGH ALONG THE WAY ARE WHAT KEEP YOU SANE. ALTHOUGH I SUPPOSE A MAN CACKLING TO HIMSELF AT A DRAWING BOARD DOESN'T LOOK ALL THAT SANE.

FASTER!

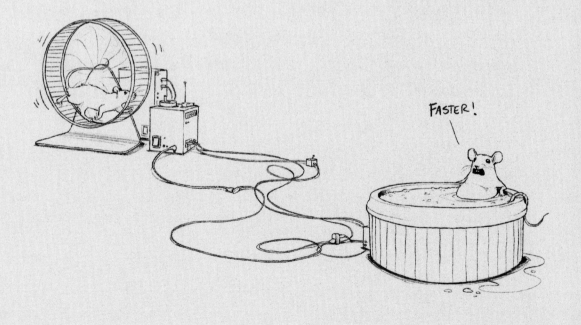

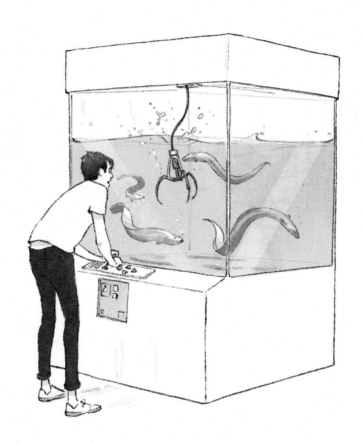

"I DON'T EVEN WANT AN EEL."

Taking The Garbage Out

"HMM, NO. CAN I TRY THE OTHER ONE AGAIN?"

"I ORDERED MY MEAL MORE THAN AN HOUR AGO! SINCE THEN,
I HAVE RECEIVED IT, EATEN IT, AND PAID FOR IT!
THANK YOU FOR A WONDERFUL EVENING!"

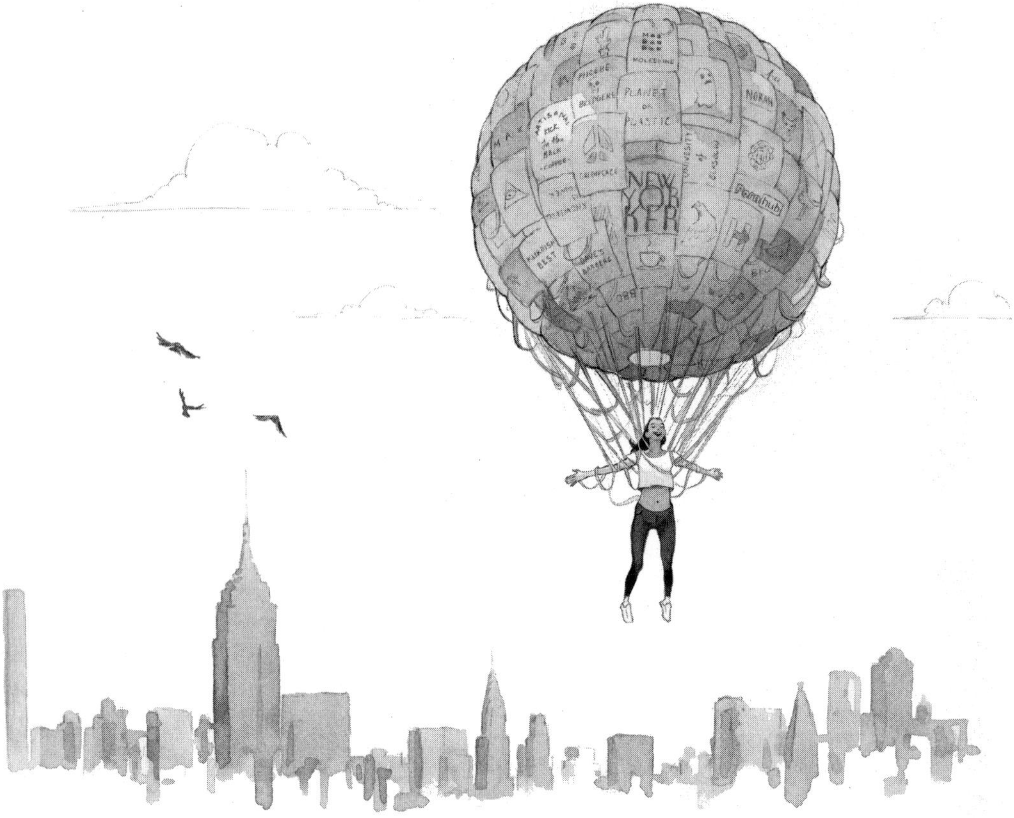
MOLESKINE
PLANET OR PLASTIC
NORAH
NEW YOR KER
Pornhub
DAVE'S BARBERS

"TOO MANY TOTE BAGS, THEY SAID."

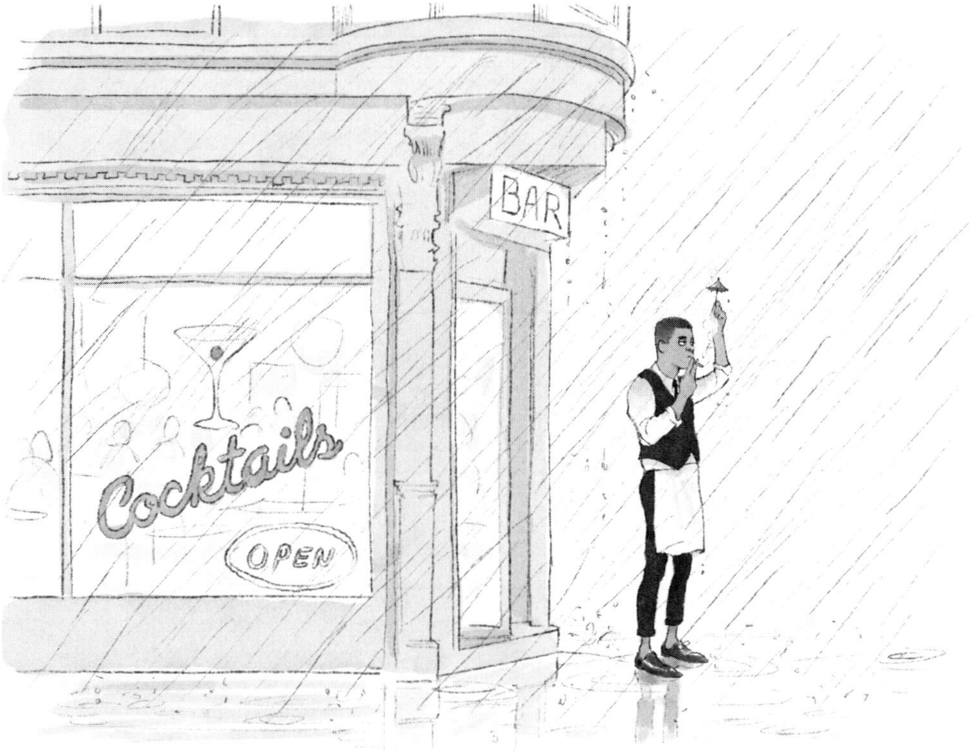
BAR
Cocktails
OPEN

"OH! SAD! SAD MAN! MAN WHO IS SAD!
SAD MAN WHO IS SAD INSIDE!"

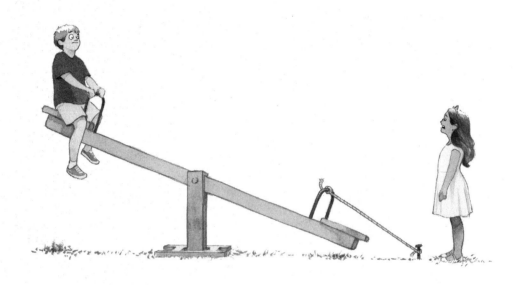

"GOODBYE, MALCOLM. GOODBYE FOREVER."

"WELL, THEN GET A BIGGER PIANO."

"SOLD! OR, GUILTY! WHERE AM I?"

"YOU WERE LUCKY. IF THE BULLET HAD BEEN AN INCH
TO THE LEFT, AND THREE INCHES LOWER, AND IT WASN'T
A BULLET, IT WAS A SHARK, AND YOU WERE A SEAL PUP,
AND THIS ALL HAPPENED IN THE OCEAN, THEN WE
MIGHT NOT BE HAVING THIS DISCUSSION."

"LEAVE THE BOTTLE."

"OK, YOU'VE PRETTY MUCH NAILED D MINOR."

"HELP! I CAN'T SWIM! NO IMMEDIATE DANGER,
BUT IT DOES WORRY ME."

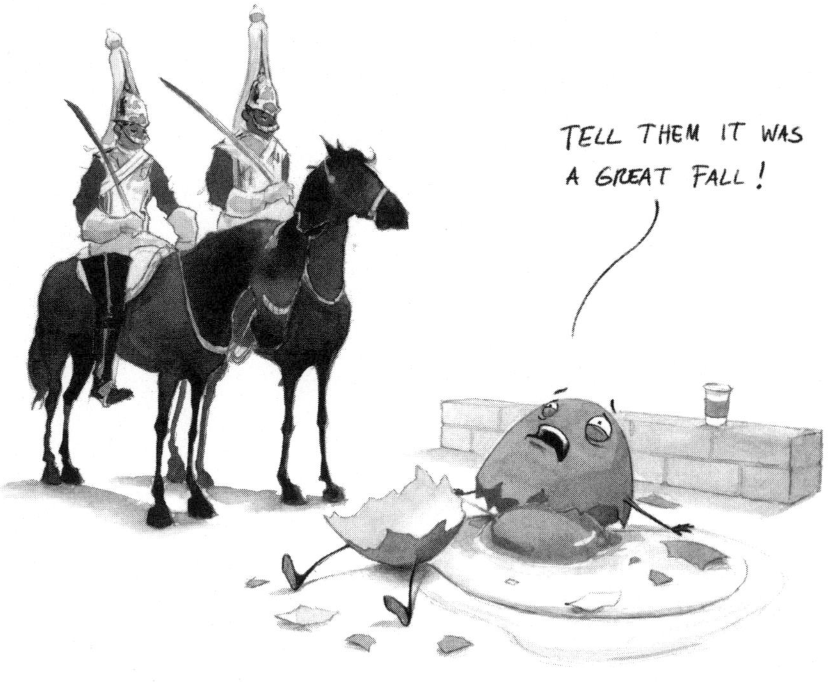
TELL THEM IT WAS
A GREAT FALL!

"ACTUALLY, IT ALL MAKES ME FEEL STATISTICALLY
AVERAGE-SIZED, AND I RESENT THE TONE."

"WHY WOULD I WANT TO BRING A HOT DOG
INTO THIS MESSED-UP WORLD?"

"YOUR X-RAYS ARE KIND OF DEPRESSING, SO HERE'S SUSAN
AND ME IN FRONT OF THE EIFFEL TOWER."

"ARE THE EYES SUPPOSED TO FOLLOW YOU HOME?"

"LISTEN, LADY—YOU ORDERED IT DRUNK,
I'M DELIVERING IT DRUNK."

"SHOES OFF?"

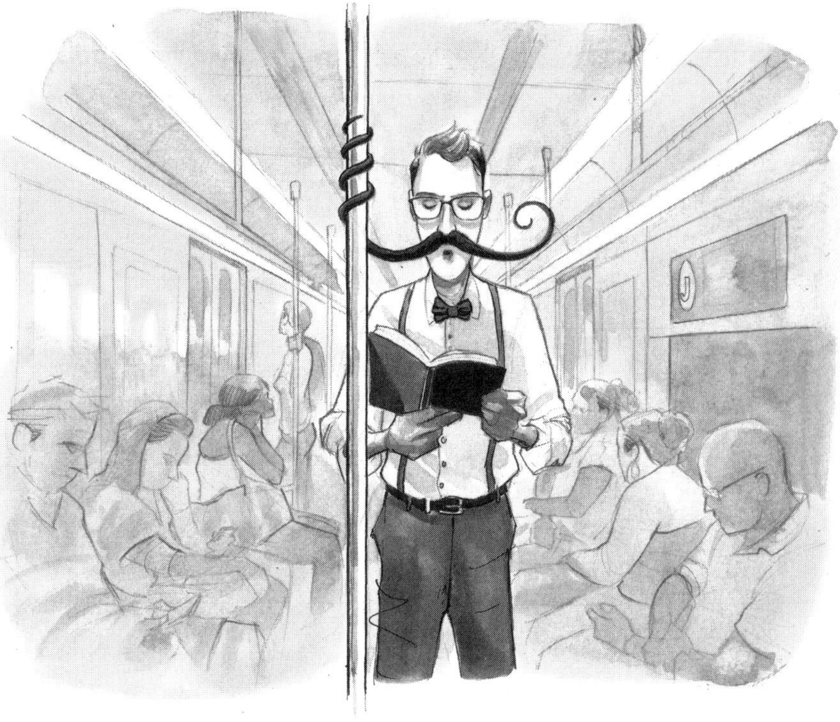
J

"WHERE DO YOU SEE YOURSELF IN TEN MISSISSIPPIS?"

"TREAD LIGHTLY, MOTHER.
THIS IS A VERY FORMATIVE TIME FOR ME."

"IT WAS SO SUDDEN."

"NO, THE OTHER ONE. NEXT TO THE SPOONS."

"LISTEN, I'M A NICE GUY AND I WANNA HELP YOU,
BUT MY FRIEND SUSIE HERE, SHE'S A LITTLE CRAZY."

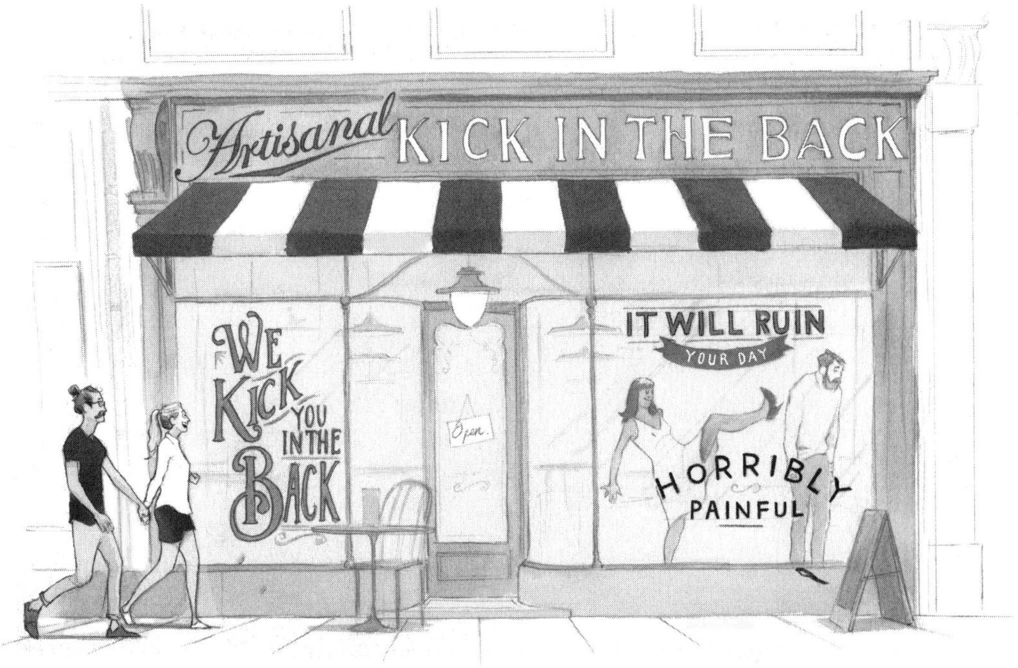
Artisanal KICK IN THE BACK
WE KICK YOU IN THE BACK
Open.
IT WILL RUIN
YOUR DAY
HORRIBLY
PAINFUL

"OOH! ARTISANAL!"

"IT RUINS THE EFFECT IF I SAY WHO IT IS.
CAN YOU JUST COME DOWN?"

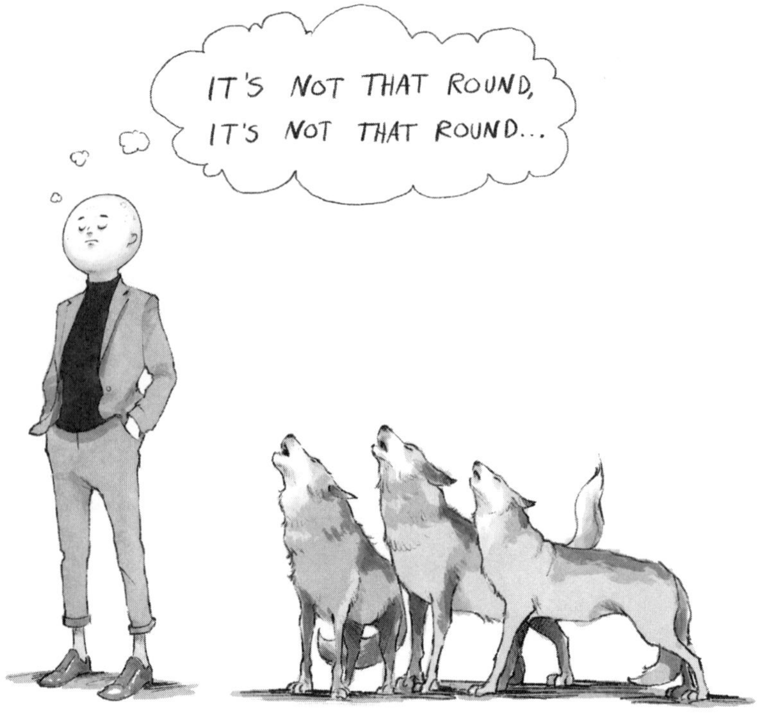
IT'S NOT THAT ROUND,
IT'S NOT THAT ROUND...

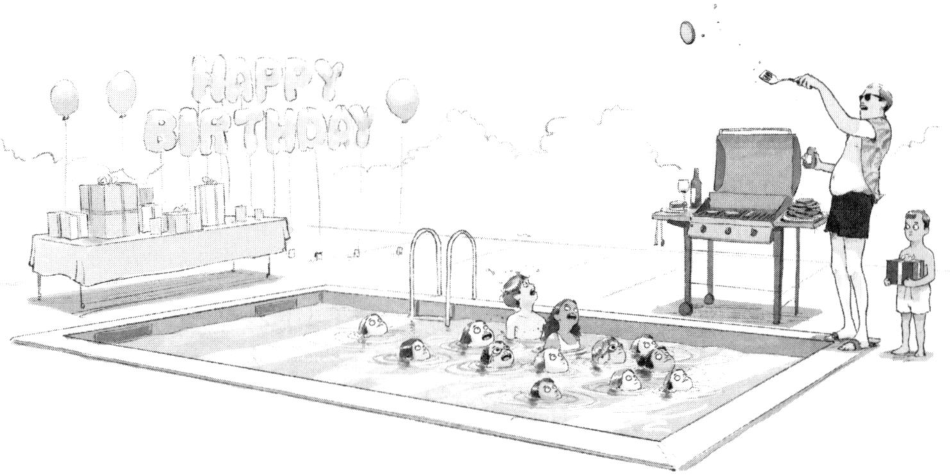
HAPPY
BIRTHDAY

"GET IN, TOBY. IT'S FEEDIN' TIME."

MY ONE LONG HAIR

Thank you

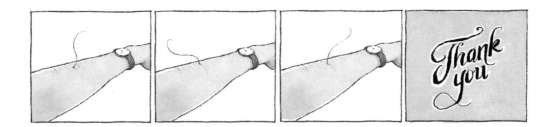

"IT'S OVER, SUSIE. YOU'RE IT."

"WHO HAD TWELVE TEQUILA BODY SHOTS?"

"HEY, CAN YOU KEEP IT DOWN?"

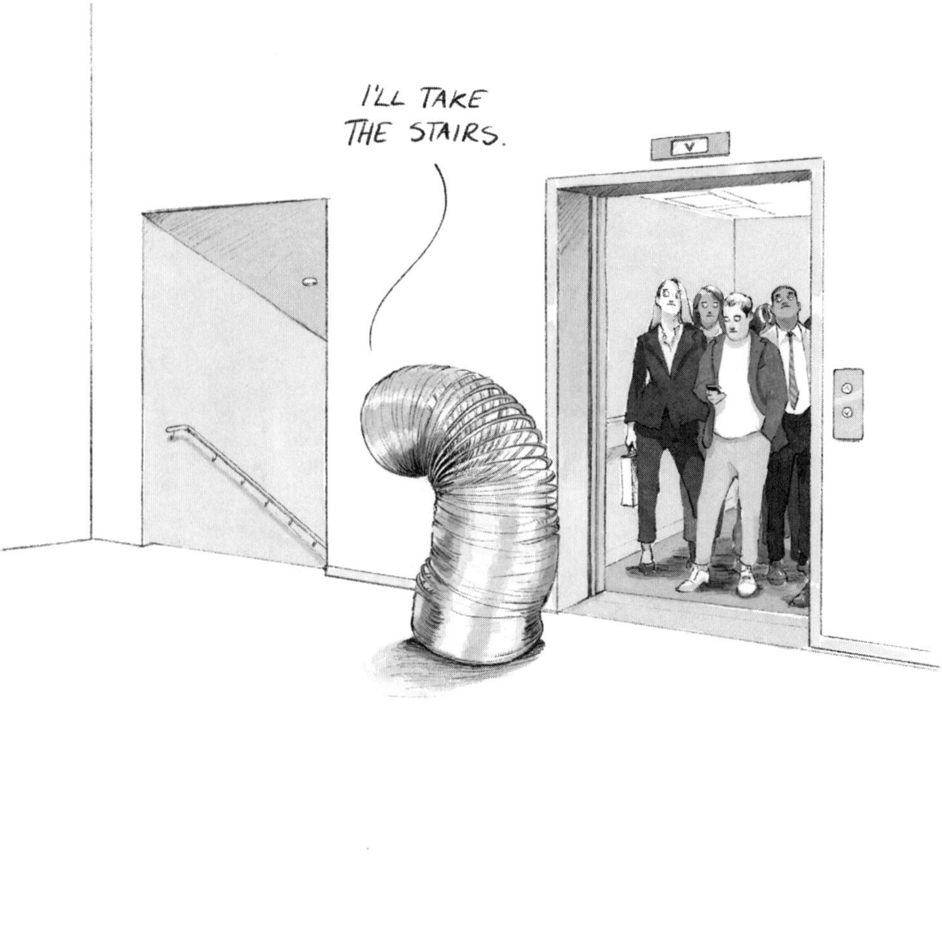
I'LL TAKE THE STAIRS.

"IS NOW A GOOD TIME TO RUN THAT IDEA BY YOU?"

141

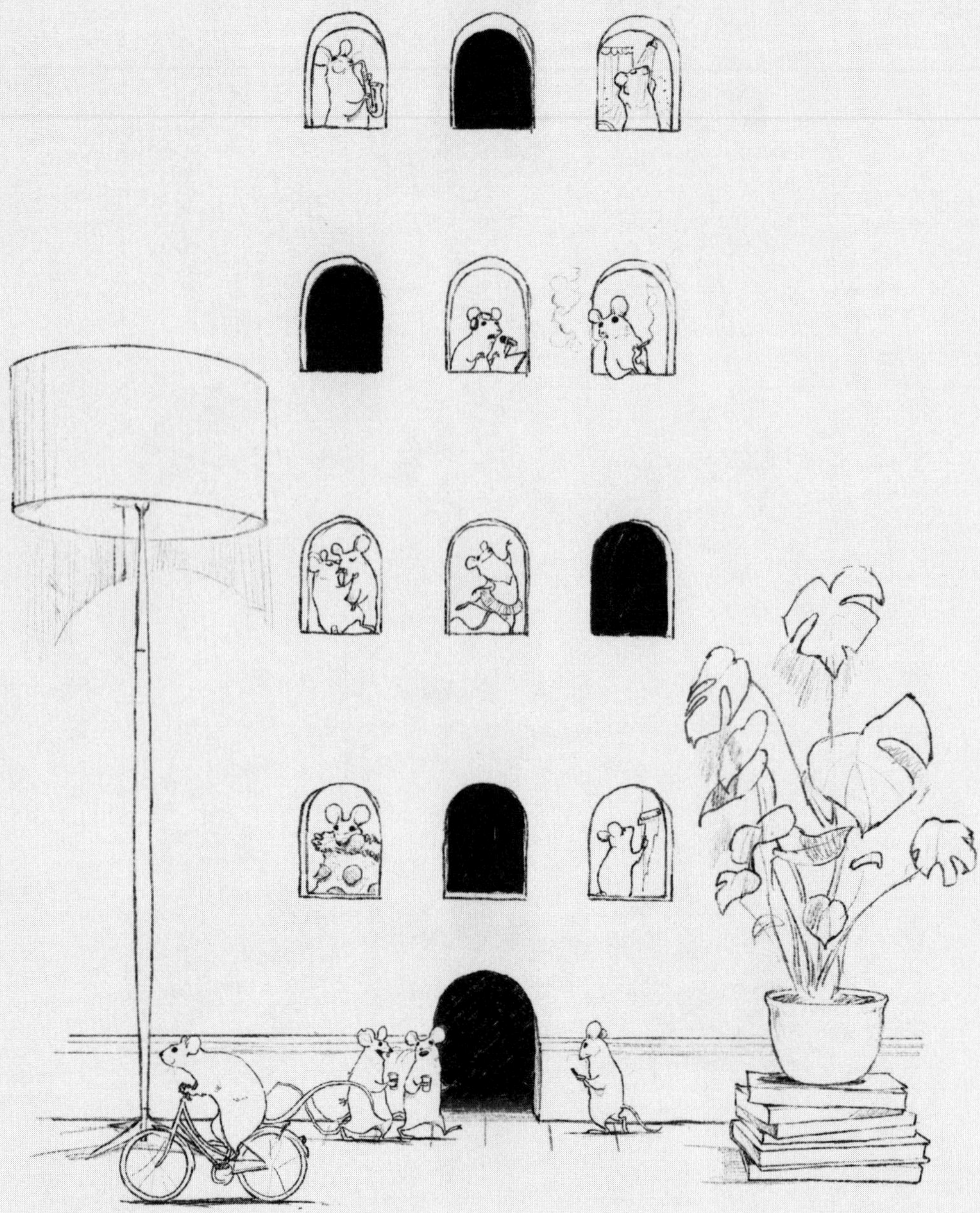

5

LIFE

IMAGINE ME, MOLESKINE IN HAND, WANDERING AROUND THIS EARTH AND JOTTING DOWN ALL THE STUFF THAT HAPPENS TO ME. TRAGIC, ISN'T IT?

WELL, I LIKE IT.

AND I RESENT YOUR TONE, ACTUALLY. FOR WHAT IS THE POINT OF LIFE IF NOT TO DISSOCIATE FROM IT ENTIRELY AND THEN TURN IT INTO CONTENT?

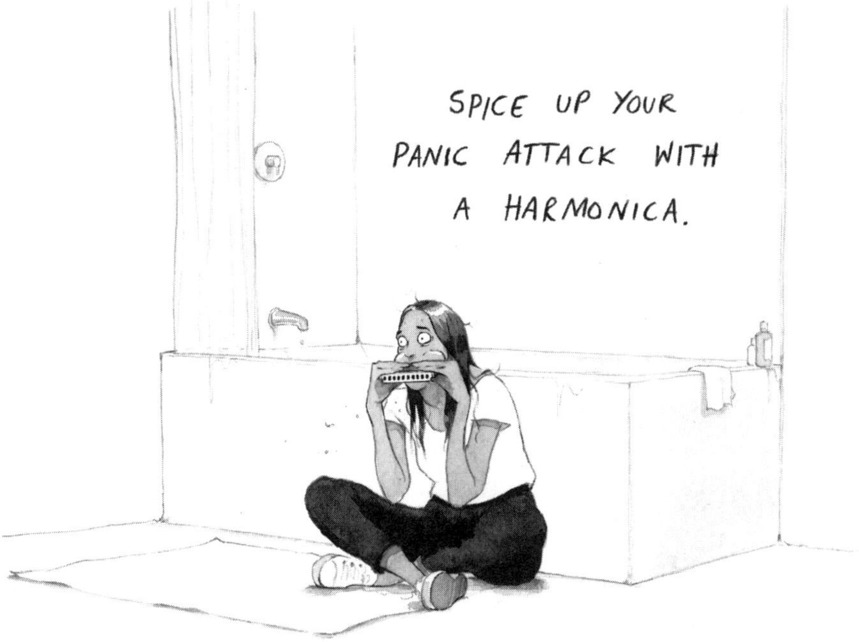
SPICE UP YOUR
PANIC ATTACK WITH
A HARMONICA.

THE ONE YOU
CAN AFFORD.

THE ONE YOU
WANT.

THE ONE YOU WOULD WANT
IF YOU COULD AFFORD THE
ONE YOU WANT.

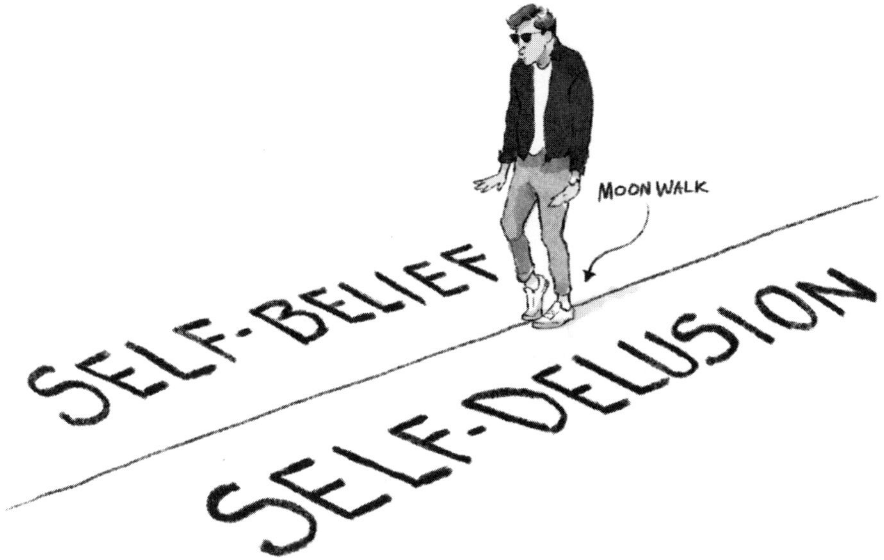
MOON WALK
SELF-BELIEF
SELF-DELUSION

"WELL, THIS CONVERSATION ISN'T GOING TO END ITSELF."

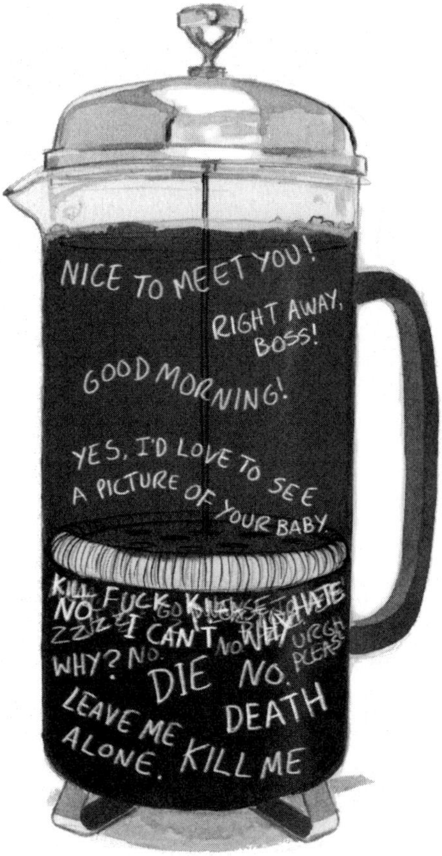
NICE TO MEET YOU!
RIGHT AWAY, BOSS!
GOOD MORNING!
YES, I'D LOVE TO SEE A PICTURE OF YOUR BABY.
KILL FUCK KILL HATE
NO
I CAN'T
WHY
URGH
WHY? NO.
DIE NO.
LEAVE ME ALONE.
DEATH
KILL ME

"HERE COMES THE AIRPLANE."

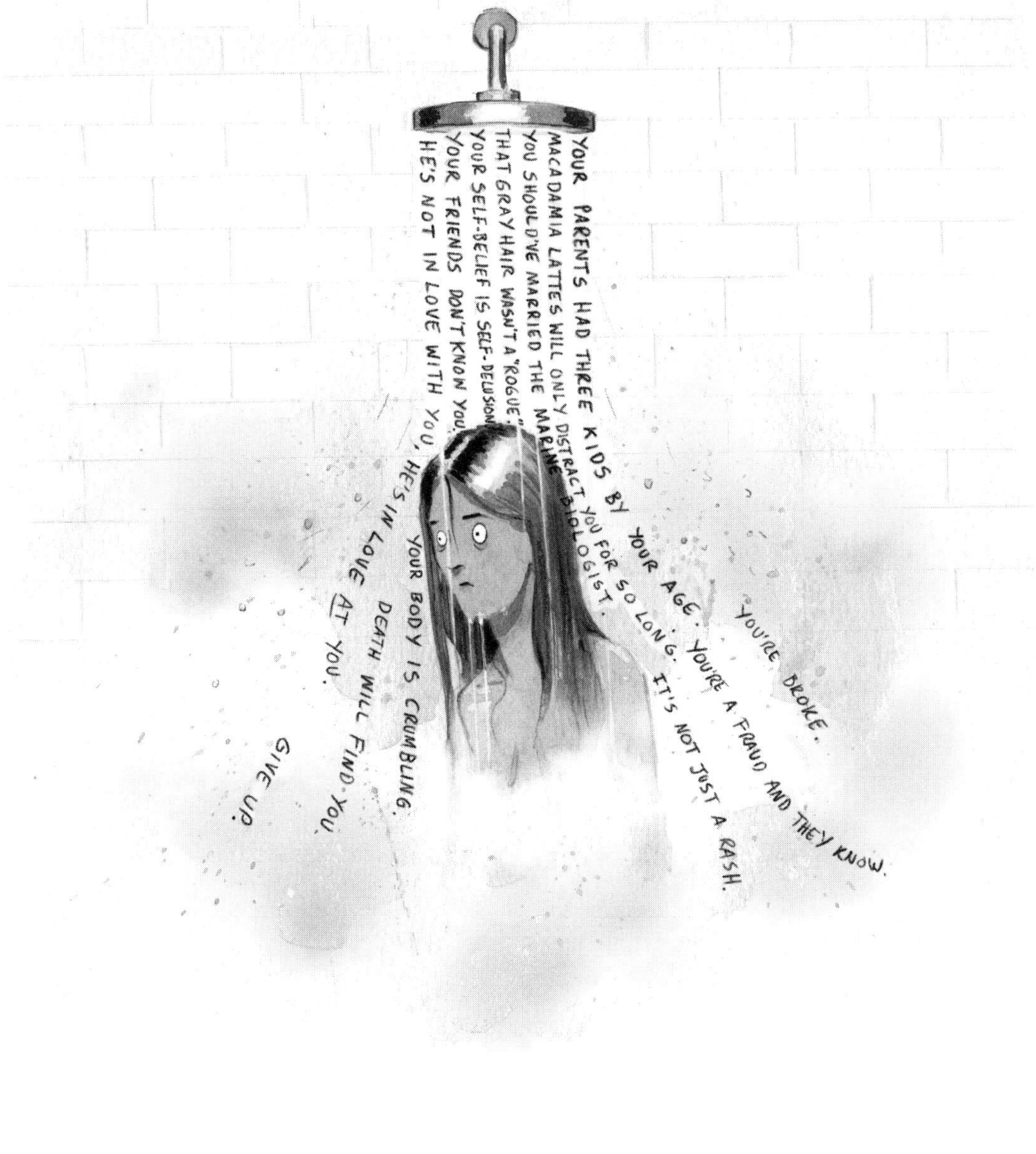
YOUR PARENTS HAD THREE KIDS BY YOUR AGE.
MACADAMIA LATTES WILL ONLY DISTRACT YOU FOR SO LONG.
YOU SHOULD'VE MARRIED THE MARINE BIOLOGIST.
THAT GRAY HAIR WASN'T A "ROGUE."
YOUR SELF-BELIEF IS SELF-DELUSION.
YOUR FRIENDS DON'T KNOW YOU.
HE'S NOT IN LOVE WITH YOU, HE'S IN LOVE AT YOU.
YOU'RE BROKE.
YOU'RE A FRAUD AND THEY KNOW.
IT'S NOT JUST A RASH.
YOUR BODY IS CRUMBLING.
DEATH WILL FIND YOU.
GIVE UP.

"ONE MORE THING—CAN YOU FIND OUT
WHY I'M SAD ALL THE TIME?"

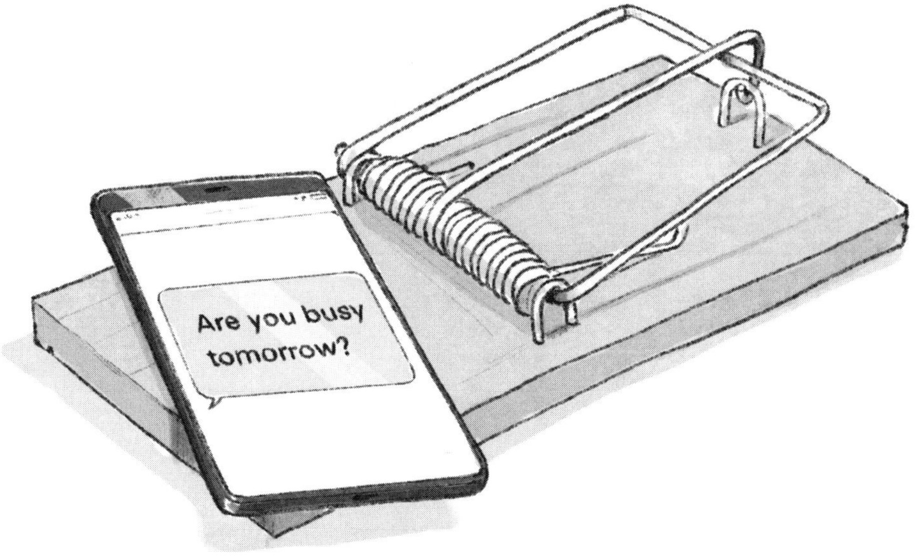
Are you busy tomorrow?

PREVIOUSLY ON... THAT BOOK YOU'VE
BEEN READING FOR THREE MONTHS

EVERY VIDEO CALL

"I SEE, AND HAVE YOU TRIED WORRYING ABOUT IT?"

ATTACK
OF THE
STRANGER'S
SHOWER
CURTAIN

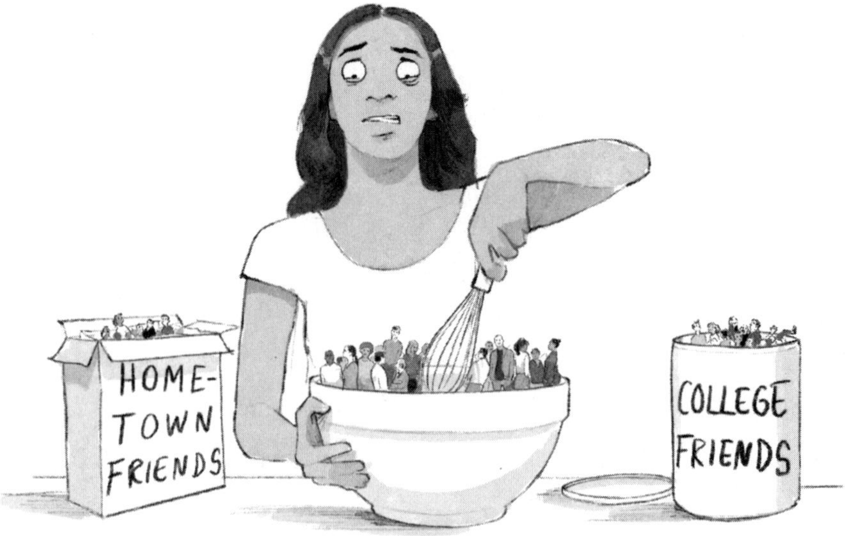
HOME-
TOWN
FRIENDS
COLLEGE
FRIENDS

NIGHT OF THE NOT KNOWING WHAT TO SAY AFTER INHALING HELIUM

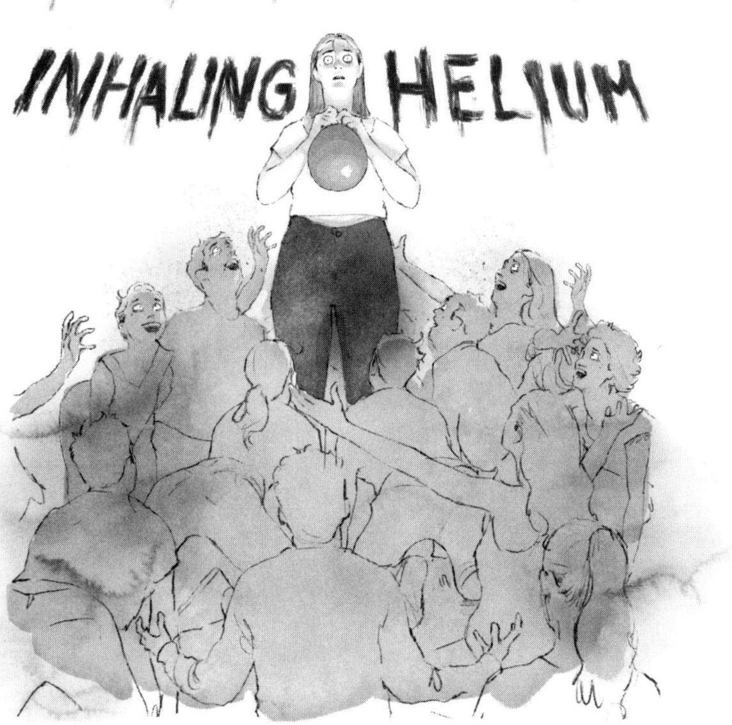

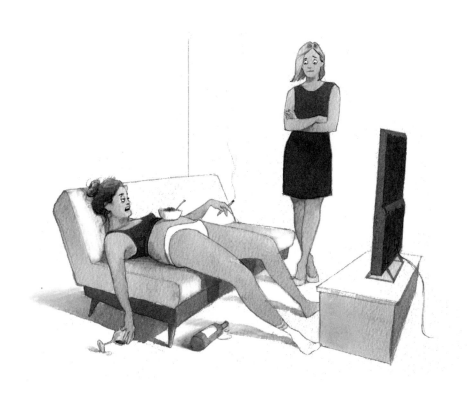

"I'M BETWEEN REASONS RIGHT NOW."

"VODKA TONIC. HOLD THE VODKA, HOLD THE TONIC,
AND HOLD MY HAND."

"CAN I GET A COFFEE AND A RELATABLE PROTAGONIST?"

"WHEN I WAS YOUR AGE, THINGS WERE HARD
FOR MY DAD WHEN HE WAS MY AGE."

"EXCUSE ME, CAN YOU WATCH MY STUFF?
AND ALSO FIGHT A THIEF?"

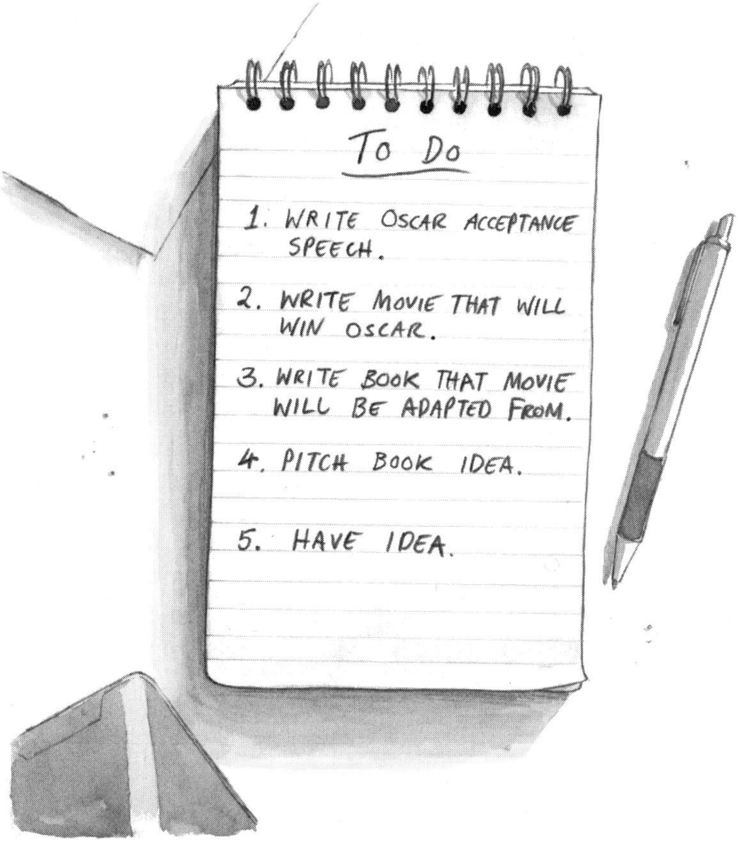
TO DO
1. WRITE OSCAR ACCEPTANCE SPEECH.
2. WRITE MOVIE THAT WILL WIN OSCAR.
3. WRITE BOOK THAT MOVIE WILL BE ADAPTED FROM.
4. PITCH BOOK IDEA.
5. HAVE IDEA.

"OH, NO. WE'RE STILL US."

HIGH ON CANCELED PLANS

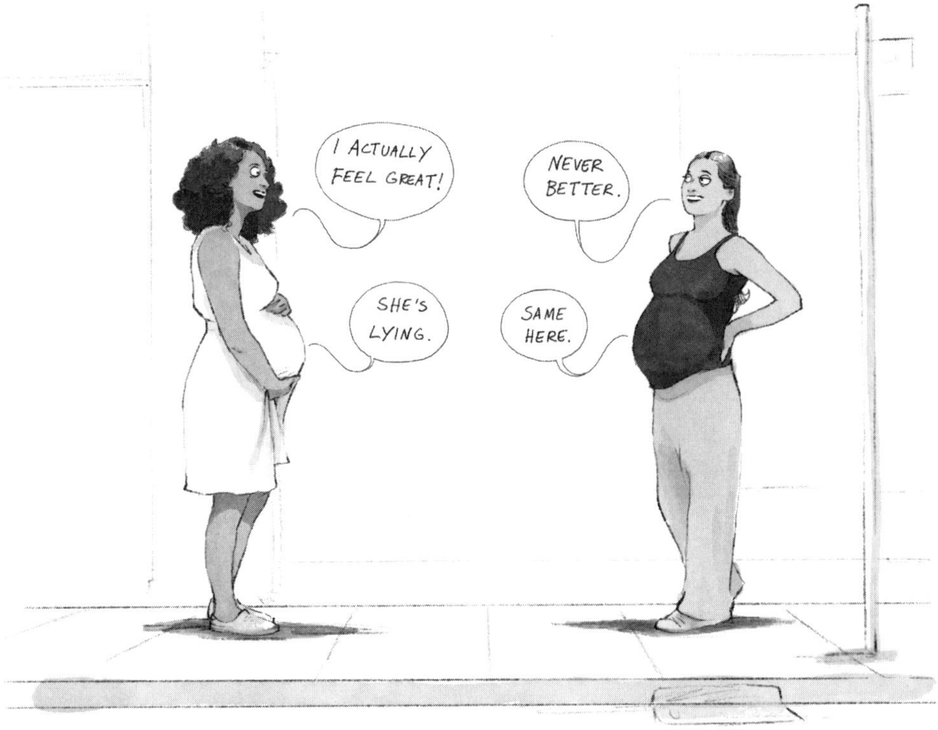
I ACTUALLY FEEL GREAT!
SHE'S LYING.
NEVER BETTER.
SAME HERE.

"SOMETIMES THE READING NOOK CAN BE A SCREAMING NOOK, OK?"

DEATH FINDS A SIGNATURE LOOK

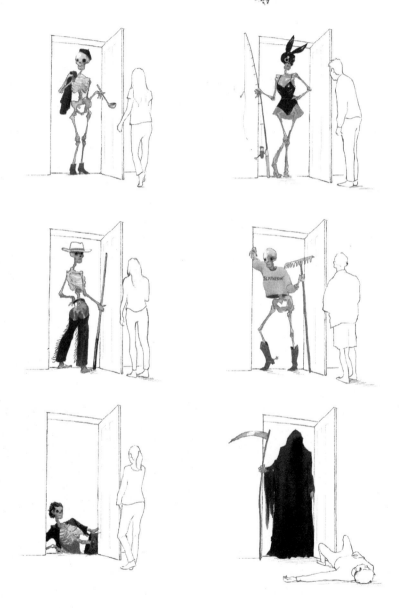

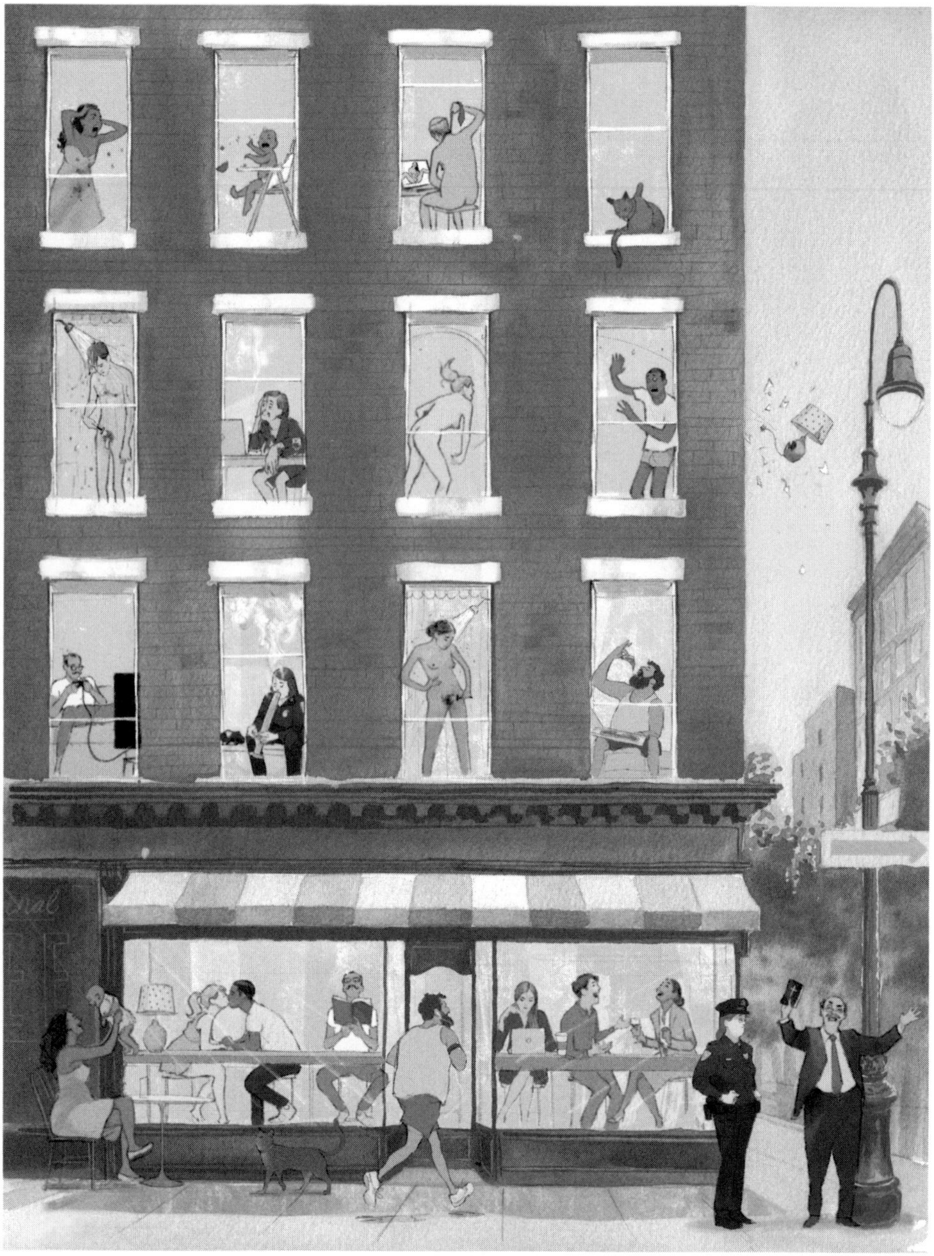

"SORRY I'M LATE. I'VE BEEN WALKING AROUND THE
BLOCK SO THAT I WOULDN'T BE EARLY."

WAITING FOR A REPLY

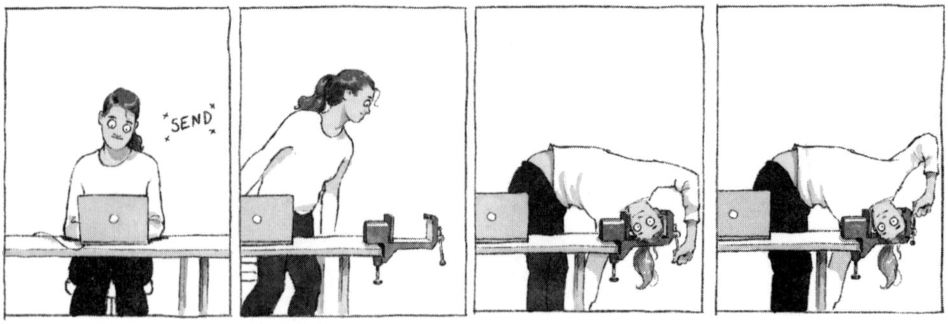
SEND

"THE USUAL?"

"I'M NOT HUNGRY. I ATE A WHOLE KEY, LIKE, A MINUTE AGO."

3rd LAW OF TODDLER DYNAMICS

Any step forward will result in an equal movement in the opposite direction.

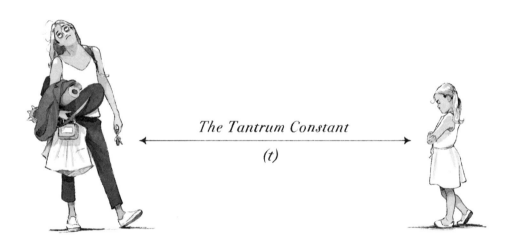

The Tantrum Constant

(t)

fig. 20.1

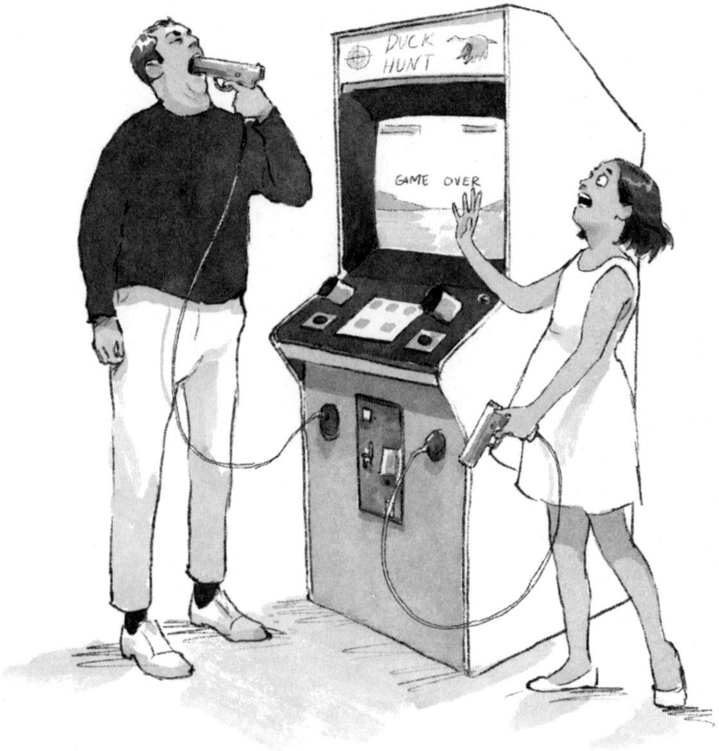
DUCK
HUNT
GAME OVER

"OK, OK, I'LL GIVE YOU A REMATCH!"

"I'VE GOT TO TAKE UP POGOING. THEY GET SO MANY BREAKS."

"SEE? IF WE'D GOTTEN THE PLACE WITH LOW CEILINGS,
WE'D BE DEAD BY NOW."

"PENCIL ME IN FOR TUESDAY, THEN ERASE IT AND
DRAW ME LYING IN BED WITH MY CHEESES."

6

LOVE

I THOUGHT I'D TRY TO EXPLAIN WHY SO MANY OF MY CARTOONS ARE ABOUT LOVE. BUT YOU GET IT. WHAT ELSE IS THERE, REALLY? IT'S THE ONLY THING WE SHOULD BE TALKING ABOUT, THINKING ABOUT, WRITING ABOUT, DRAWING ABOUT. LOVE IS THE ONLY THING WORTH DOING ANYTHING FOR.

OH, AND MONEY. MONEY IS ALSO KEY.

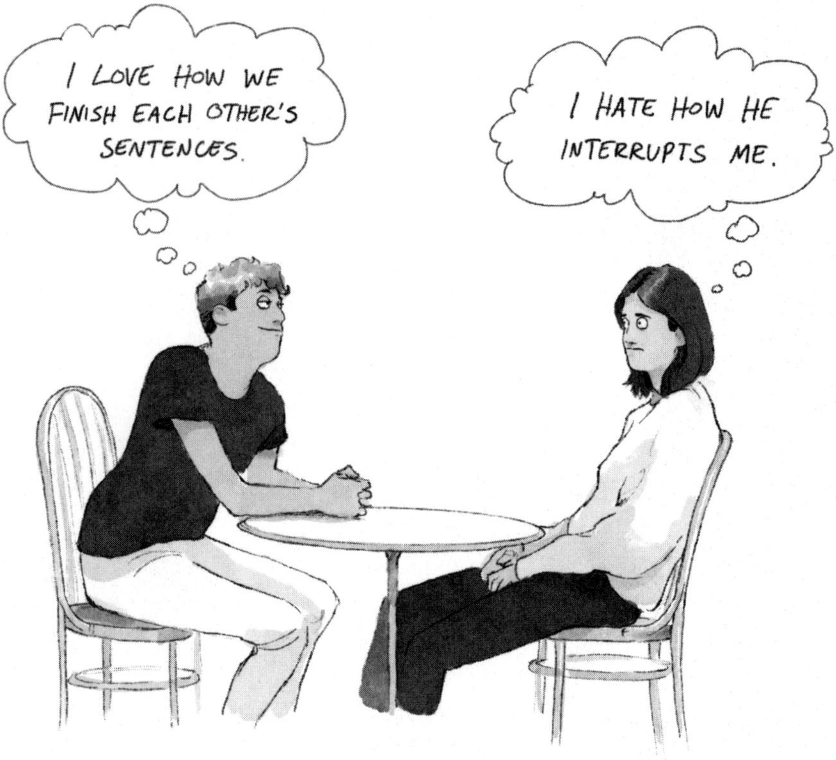
I LOVE HOW WE FINISH EACH OTHER'S SENTENCES.
I HATE HOW HE INTERRUPTS ME.

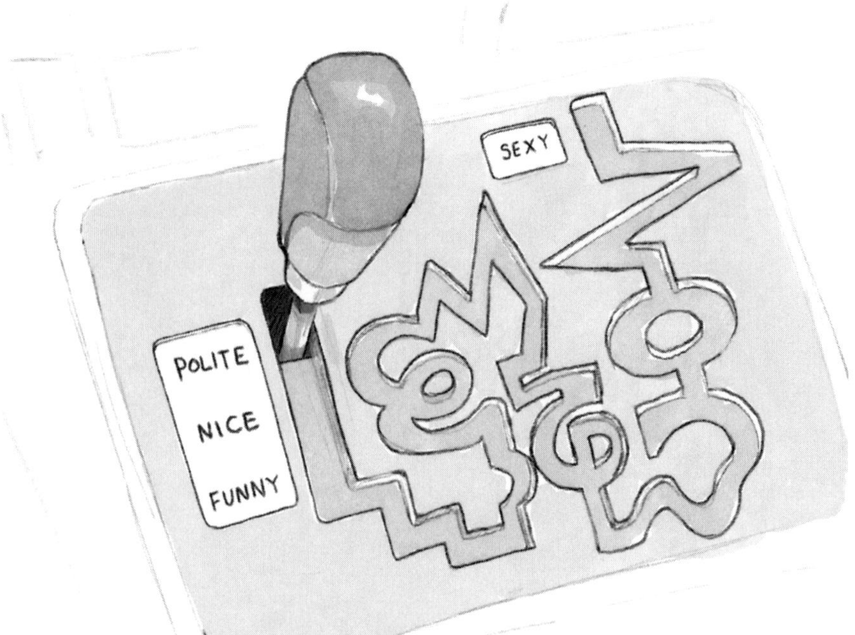
SEXY
POLITE
NICE
FUNNY

"YOUR DAD AND I ARE GETTING A DIVORCE."

Living With Rapunzel

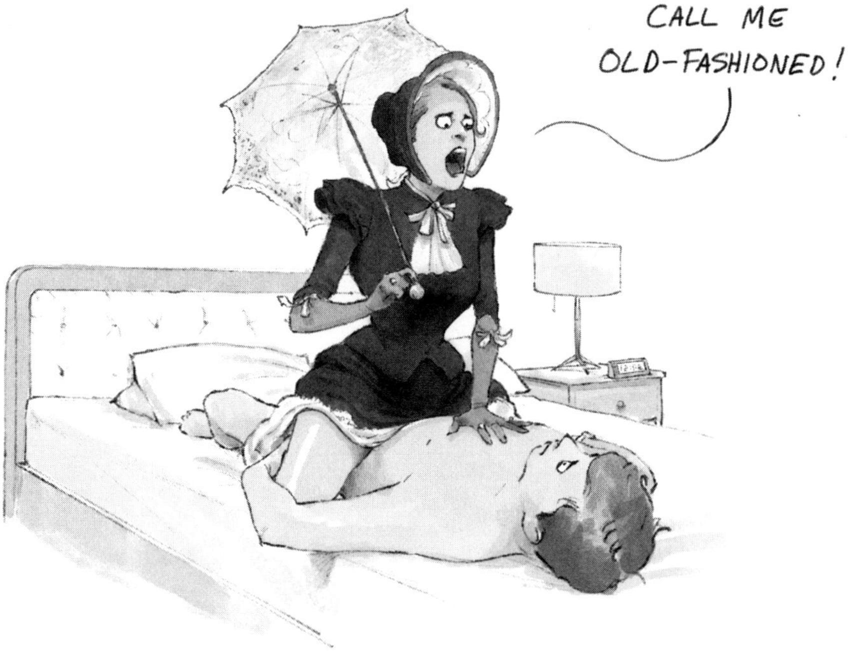
CALL ME OLD-FASHIONED!

WHERE YOUR PERSONALITIES GO WHILE YOU'RE HAVING SEX

WANNA GRAB A COFFEE?
DON'T THEY NEED US?
WE CAN TAKE A BREAK. LATTE, RIGHT?
HOW WILL THEY BE THEMSELVES WITHOUT US?
OH, THEY WON'T.
DO THEY LAUGH?
NOT WITHOUT US.

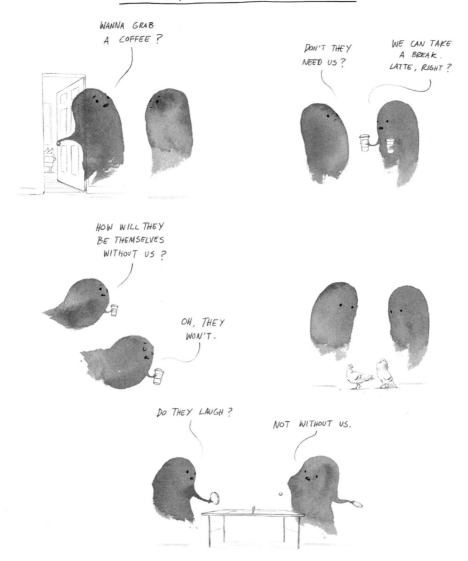

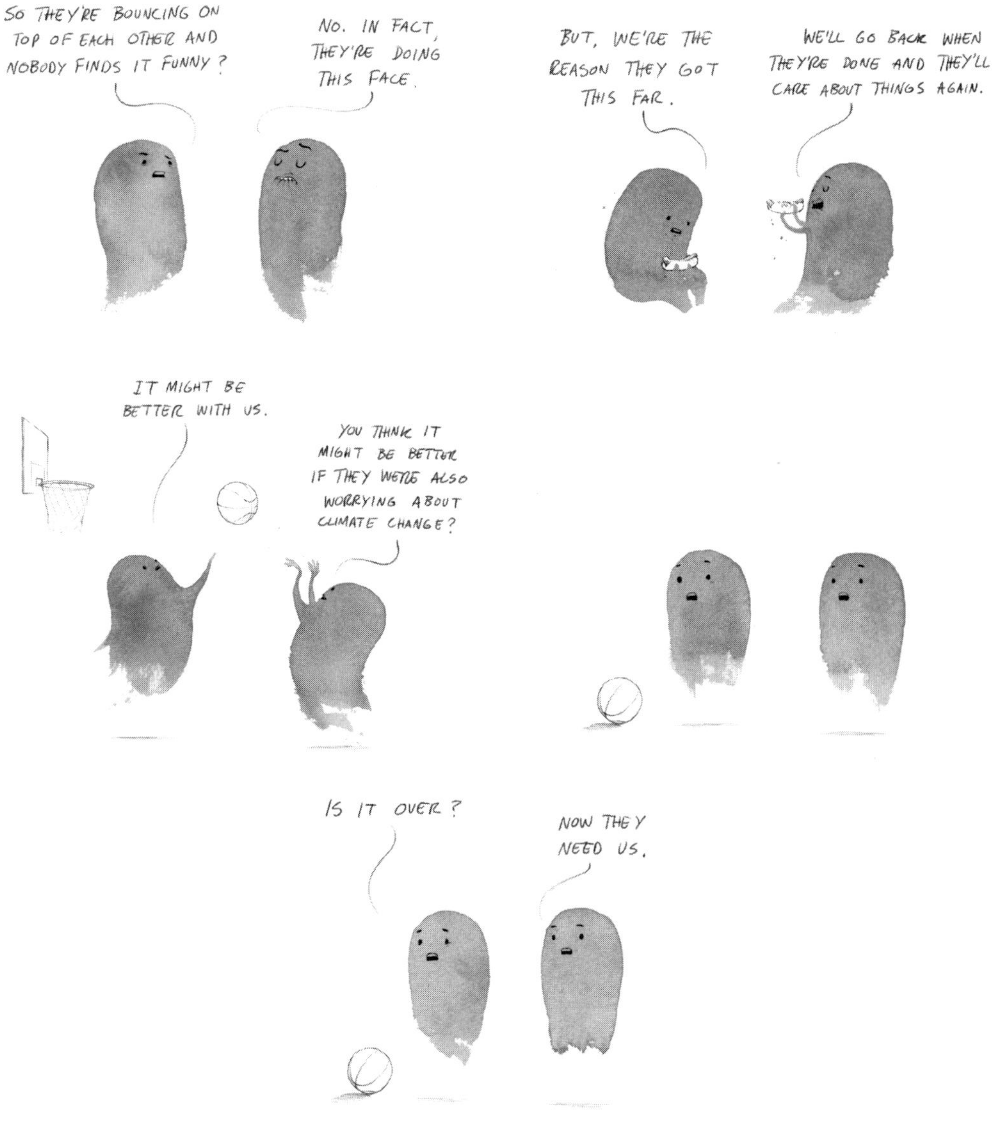
SO THEY'RE BOUNCING ON TOP OF EACH OTHER AND NOBODY FINDS IT FUNNY?
NO. IN FACT, THEY'RE DOING THIS FACE.
BUT, WE'RE THE REASON THEY GOT THIS FAR.
WE'LL GO BACK WHEN THEY'RE DONE AND THEY'LL CARE ABOUT THINGS AGAIN.
IT MIGHT BE BETTER WITH US.
YOU THINK IT MIGHT BE BETTER IF THEY WERE ALSO WORRYING ABOUT CLIMATE CHANGE?
IS IT OVER?
NOW THEY NEED US.

"THIS IS THE ONE, GUYS. THIS IS THE SUIT
I'M GOING TO GET DIVORCED IN."

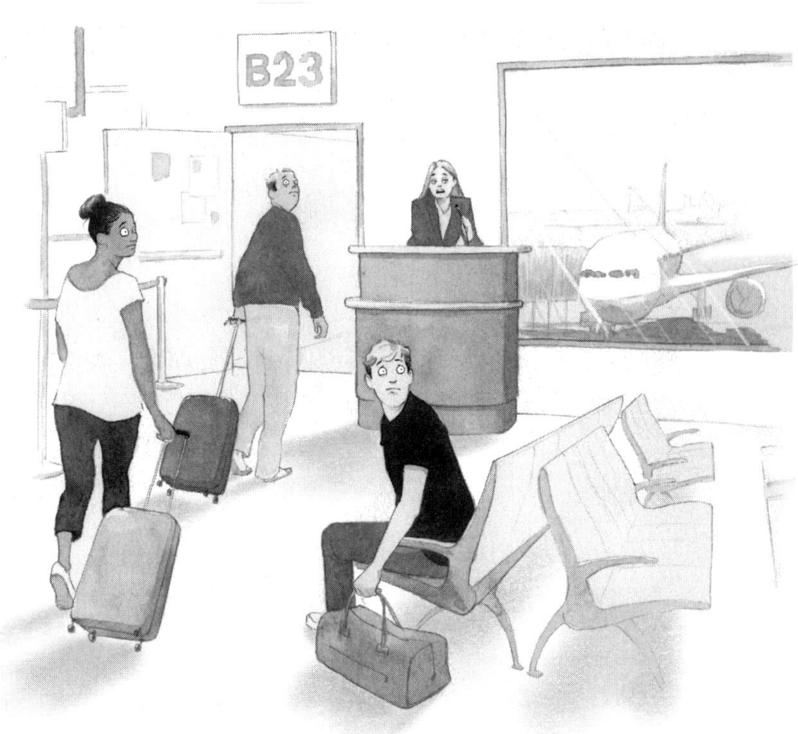
B23

"NOW BOARDING PASSENGERS DESPERATELY AWAITING THEIR ROM-COM MOMENT."

RESISTING SEX TO SAVE THE FRIEND GROUP

"PAUL? SUSAN! FROM THE GYM? I SHOWED YOU HOW TO USE THE
ELLIPTICAL? WE WENT FOR COFFEE? ONE THING LED TO
ANOTHER? WE STARTED DATING? THEN WE GOT MARRIED? WE HAD
TWO KIDS? BUT WE GOT DIVORCED? I GOT CUSTODY? YOU SEE
THEM ON THE WEEKENDS? BUT YOU WANT THEM CHRISTMAS? I
SAID NO WAY? YOU CALLED ME LAST NIGHT IN TEARS? SUSAN!"

"IGNORE THEM."

"AS YOU CAN SEE, THE ROOM COMES WITH A MURPHY BED
AND A MURPHY BOYFRIEND."

"NO, I ORDERED THE LIFETIME OF DOING WHATEVER I WANT."

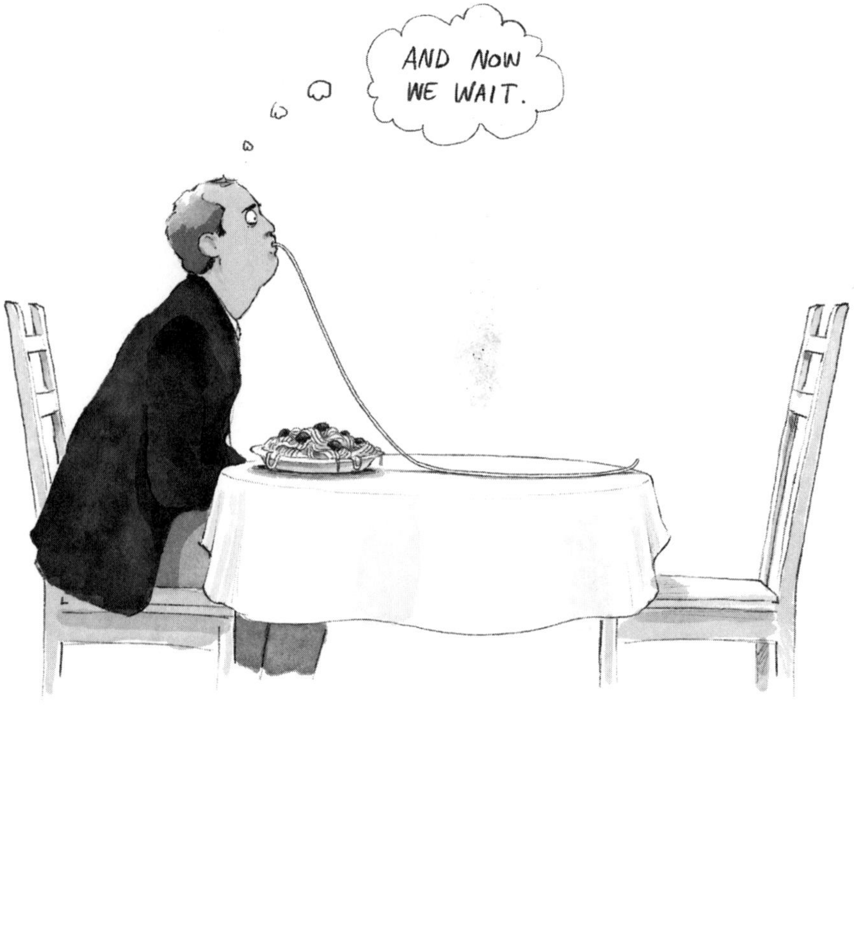
AND NOW WE WAIT.

"I'M ASHAMED OF IT ALL, TO BE HONEST."

"I'VE MET SOMEONE ELSE."

"QUIT HOGGING THE SHEETS, LOVELESS VOID!"

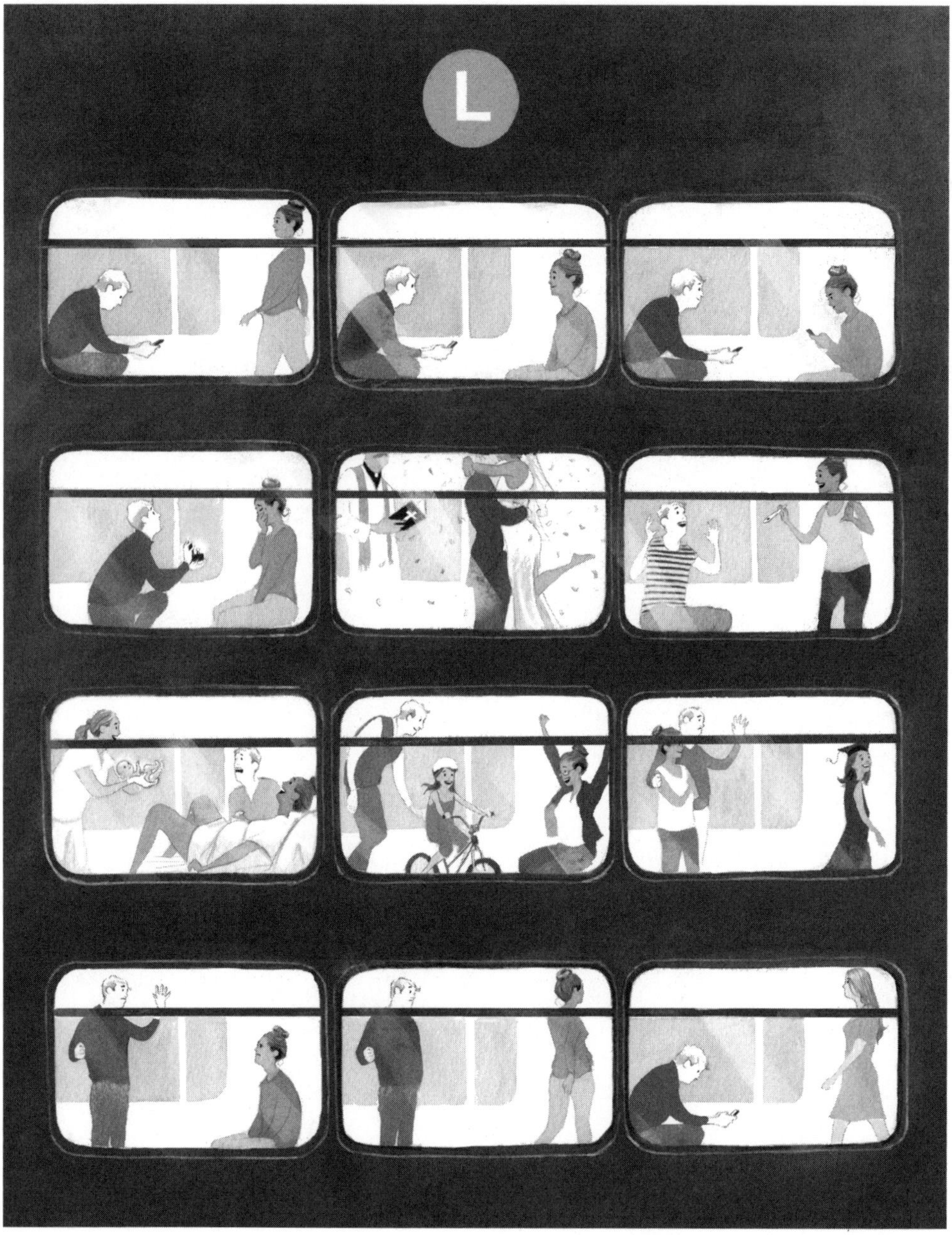
L

RAPUNZEL ON THE DATING APPS

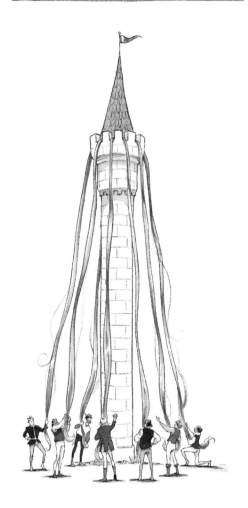

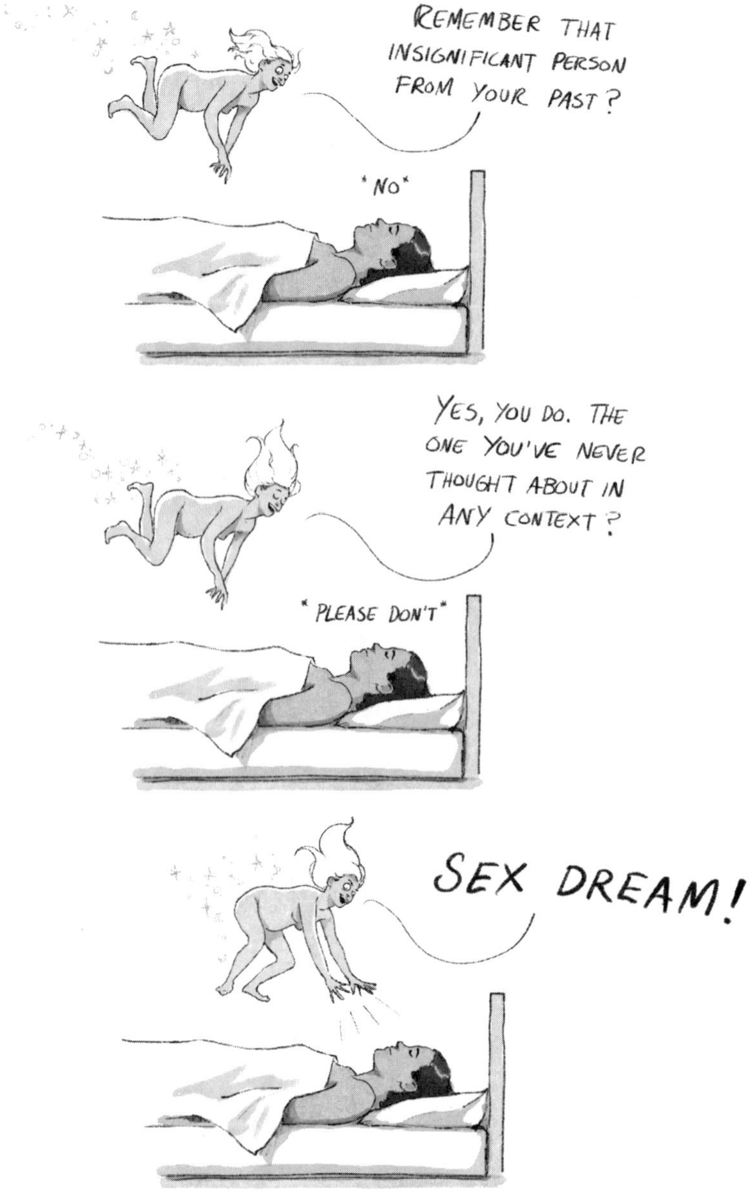
REMEMBER THAT INSIGNIFICANT PERSON FROM YOUR PAST?
NO
YES, YOU DO. THE ONE YOU'VE NEVER THOUGHT ABOUT IN ANY CONTEXT?
PLEASE DON'T
SEX DREAM!

"DON'T HOLD BACK."

"I'M GETTING OAK, CHERRIES, AND THE URGE TO TELL
MY EX THAT WE MADE A MISTAKE."

"SORRY, I JUST REALIZED I'M GONNA DIE ONE DAY."

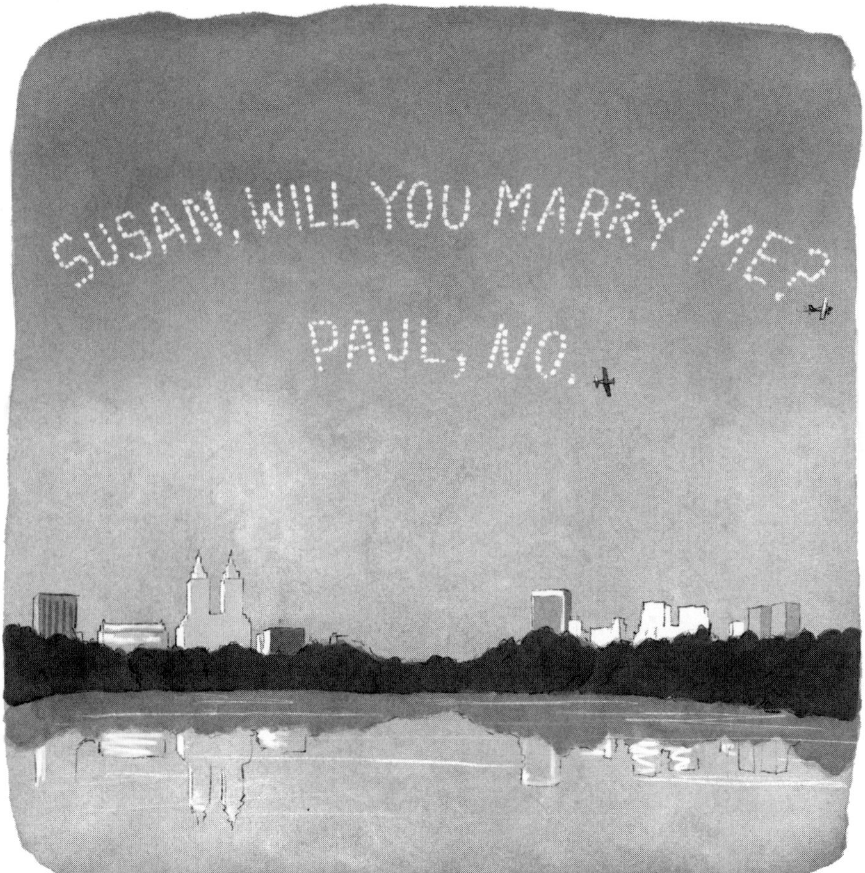
SUSAN, WILL YOU MARRY ME?
PAUL, NO.

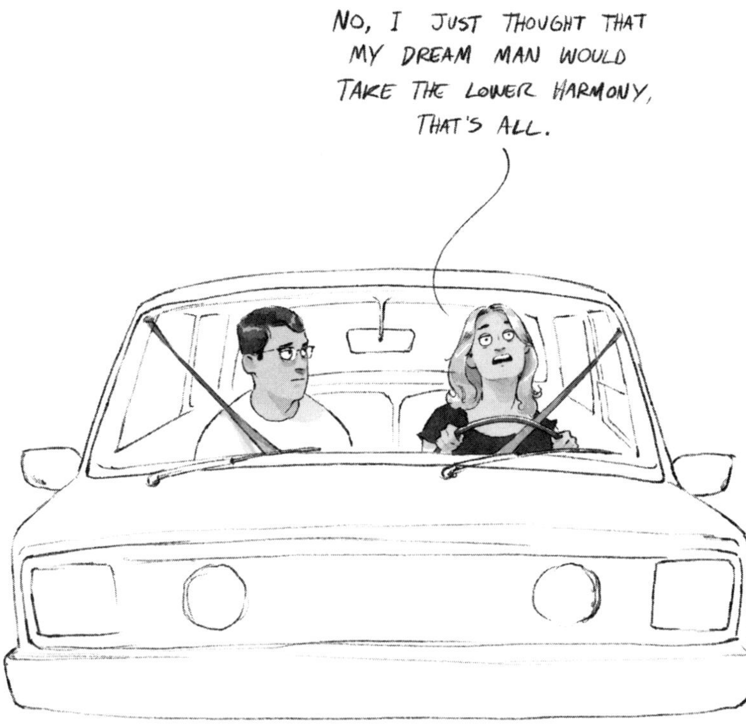
NO, I JUST THOUGHT THAT MY DREAM MAN WOULD TAKE THE LOWER HARMONY, THAT'S ALL.

"EXCUSE ME, I HATE TO COMPLAIN, BUT MY HUSBAND
IS AWFUL AND I'M DEEPLY UNHAPPY."

"YOU'RE CONFUSING US HAVING CHEMISTRY
WITH ME BEING FUNNY."

THE ADVENTURES OF
LADY NO-KIDS

"ANYWAY, I'M GONNA FOLLOW THIS GOOSE FOR A WHILE
AND SEE WHERE I END UP."

CONTINUED...

WHY DOESN'T SHE HAVE ANY CHILDREN?
I DON'T THINK SHE WANTS ANY.

WHY NOT?
I DON'T KNOW. YOU'D HAVE TO ASK HER.

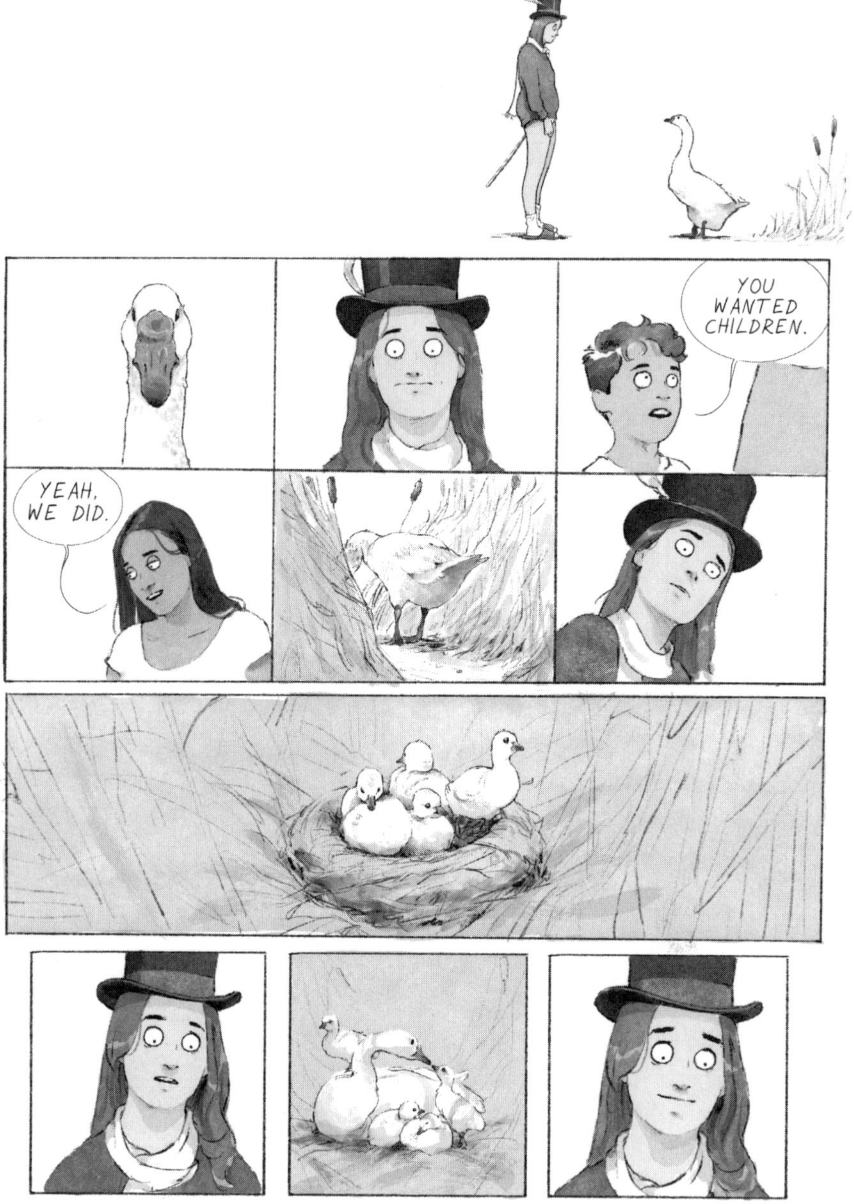
YOU WANTED CHILDREN.
YEAH, WE DID.

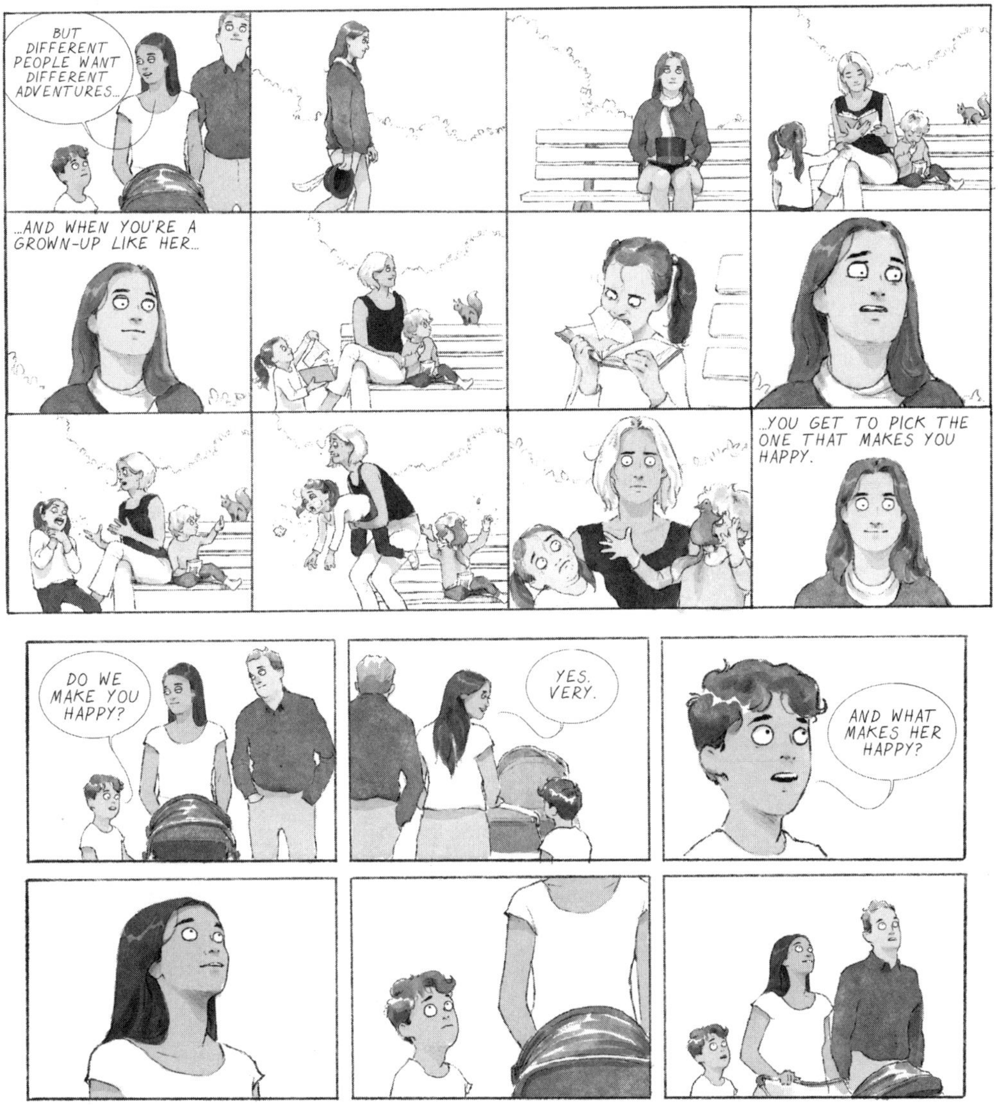
BUT DIFFERENT PEOPLE WANT DIFFERENT ADVENTURES...
...AND WHEN YOU'RE A GROWN-UP LIKE HER...
...YOU GET TO PICK THE ONE THAT MAKES YOU HAPPY.
DO WE MAKE YOU HAPPY?
YES. VERY.
AND WHAT MAKES HER HAPPY?

ACKNOWLEDGMENTS

THANK YOU TO THE NEW YORKER. I'LL NEVER FORGET WHEN THEY RAN MY FIRST CARTOON. I WAS SO DIABOLICALLY PROUD TO BE IN AN ISSUE OF THE MAGAZINE THAT WHEN I SAW A GUY READING IT ON THE TRAIN, I MISSED MY STATION BY, LIKE, THREE STOPS BECAUSE I WANTED TO SEE HIM SEE MY CARTOON. WHEN HE FINALLY ARRIVED ON THE PAGE THAT I HAD SPENT THE LAST WEEK STARING AT IN DISBELIEF, HE SCANNED DOWN TO MY DRAWING, EXHALED A JOYLESS PUFF OF AIR FROM HIS NOSE, AND THEN TURNED THE PAGE.

YEARS HAVE PASSED SINCE THEN, AND ALTHOUGH THAT MAN IS NOW MYSTERIOUSLY DEAD, THE SURREAL THRILL OF SEEING MY WORK IN THOSE PAGES IS STILL VERY MUCH ALIVE! I WANT TO THANK EVERYONE AT THE MAGAZINE—PARTICULARLY EMMA ALLEN, COLIN STOKES, AND DAVID REMNICK—FOR SHIELDING THE WORLD FROM MY TERRIBLE IDEAS AND SHOWING IT THE GOOD ONES.

THANK YOU TO THE GREAT ESTHER NEWBERG, MY TIRELESS AND TREMENDOUS AGENT. IT IS ENTIRELY THANKS TO YOU, AND OUR BELOVED HEATHER KARPAS, THAT I HAVE THE OPPORTUNITY TO WRITE THESE BOOKS. IN SHORT? IT'S ALL YOUR FAULT.

GORDON WISE, YOU MAKE NAVIGATING THE TREACHEROUS PATHS OF PUBLISHING SEEM SO EASY. THANK YOU FOR BEING MY LITERARY SHERPA. THANK YOU TO LOUISE COURT, CHARLOTTE HUMPHERY, AND EVERYONE AT SCEPTRE. YOU'VE MADE ME FEEL COMPLETELY AT HOME IN A WORLD I KNOW NOTHING ABOUT.

THANK YOU TO EVERYONE AT MARINER BOOKS—PARTICULARLY IVY GIVENS, CHLOE FOSTER, AND BRIAN MOORE, FOR ALL YOUR SKILLFUL WORK ON THE INTERIOR, THE DESIGN, AND THE COVER. AND THANKS ESPECIALLY TO MY FEARLESS EDITOR, DAVID ROSENTHAL. I CANNOT BELIEVE WE GOT THROUGH TWO WHOLE BOOKS WITHOUT ONE OF US GETTING FIRED. THANK YOU FOR ALL YOUR BELIEF AND GUIDANCE, MY FRIEND.

MY FAMILY AND FRIENDS, I LOVE YOU ALL, AND I'LL TELL YOU TO YOUR ABSOLUTE FACES.

AND FINALLY, THANK YOU TO ALL MY LOYAL VERMIN SOLDIERS OUT THERE IN THE GUTTERS OF THE WORLD. BE PATIENT, MY CHILDREN, AND WAIT FOR MY SIGNAL.